GENERATE **PASSIVE INCOME**
WITH AI PROMPTS AND IMAGE GENERATION

THE ULTIMATE CHATGPT AND DALL-E *SIDE HUSTLE* BIBLE

WELL OVER 101 SIDE HUSTLES

MAKE MONEY, ACHIEVE FINANCIAL FREEDOM
AND **LIVE LIFE ON YOUR TERMS**

FUTUREFRONT

General Disclaimer Notice:
Please note the information contained within this document is for educational and entertainment purposes only. All effort has been expended to present accurate, up-to-date, and reliable, complete information. No warranties of any kind are declared or implied. Readers acknowledge that the author is not engaging in the rendering of legal, financial, medical or professional advice. The content within this book has been derived from various sources. Please consult a licensed professional before attempting any techniques outlined in this book. You should conduct your own research and seek professional advice as necessary to ensure the success and legality of your endeavors.

By reading this document, the reader agrees that under no circumstances is the author responsible for any losses, direct or indirect, which are incurred as a result of the use of the information contained within this document, including, but not limited to, — errors, omissions, or inaccuracies.

Earnings Disclaimer:
The potential earnings mentioned are estimates and not guarantees of income. Individual results may vary based on factors such as skill level, effort, market demand, and adherence to platform guidelines. The earnings range provided is intended to give a general idea of what some individuals may achieve, but it is not representative of typical results. Success in any endeavor often requires persistence, skill development, and a long-term commitment.

Platform Compliance:
It is crucial to follow all rules, policies, and terms of service of any platforms you use. Non-compliance can result in penalties, including but not limited to account suspension, removal of content, and forfeiture of earnings.

Ethical Considerations:
When using AI tools or other resources, it is important to maintain ethical standards by respecting copyright laws and ensuring originality in your work. If you choose to disclose AI tool usage, be transparent about your process to maintain trust and integrity with your audience and potential clients.

Non-Affiliation Disclaimer:
No affiliate links were used in this book, and we do not receive any form of payment or commissions. We do not work for, nor are we affiliated with, any specific AI tools or platforms mentioned. References to these tools and platforms are based on their publicly available features and capabilities, and any use of them should comply with their respective terms of service and guidelines. All recommendations are made impartially and are intended solely to provide helpful information to readers.

Tax Disclaimer:
Any income earned from these activities may be subject to taxes. It is your responsibility to comply with tax laws and regulations applicable in your jurisdiction. Consult a tax professional for advice specific to your situation.

Research Recommendation:
It is important to conduct your own research to determine which platforms and methods are best suited to your specific needs and goals. Each platform has unique features, policies, and potential benefits that should be thoroughly evaluated before committing to their use.

Contents

Introduction

Welcome to the AI Side Hustle Revolution

"The only limit to our realization of tomorrow is our doubts of today."

Franklin D. Roosevelt

Welcome, future AI entrepreneur! If you've picked up this book, you're likely looking for ways to boost your income and explore new opportunities, or you're simply curious about how AI can transform the way we work. Whatever your motivation, you're in the right place. How we work is changing rapidly, and artificial intelligence is at the forefront of this transformation. This book guides you in navigating and using this new landscape to your advantage.

In the following pages, we're going to explore the exciting world of AI-powered side hustles. Your guides on this journey are two powerful AI tools: ChatGPT, a versatile language model, and Dall-E, an impressive image generator. Don't worry if you're not familiar with these tools yet – by the end of this book, you'll be using them like a pro. These AI assistants are not just fancy tech toys but potential game-changers for your financial future. You will be surprised at how they can help you; whether you are designing logos or starting a dog-walking side hustle, AI can assist!

The AI Revolution in Side Hustles

Artificial Intelligence has been making headlines for years, but it's only recently become accessible enough for individuals to use in their everyday lives and work. This democratization of AI technology has opened up vast opportunities for side hustlers and entrepreneurs.

ChatGPT, developed by OpenAI, is a large language model that can understand and generate human-like text. It can help with writing, brainstorming, problem-solving, and even coding. Imagine having a tireless assistant who can help you draft articles, create marketing copy, or even help you learn new skills.

Dall-E, also from OpenAI, is an AI system that can create realistic images and art from textual descriptions. It's like having a graphic designer on call 24/7, ready to visually bring your ideas to life. From creating unique illustrations for your blog to designing merchandise for your online store, Dall-E expands the possibilities of what you can create.

Together, these tools provide a powerful combination of verbal and visual creativity to supercharge your side hustle efforts.

What This Book Offers

We'll dive into 101 creative ways you can leverage these AI tools to create income streams. There are vast and varied possibilities, from writing and design to marketing and beyond. Whether you're a creative looking for new outlets, a professional seeking to diversify your skills, or someone entirely new to side hustles, there's something here for you. Along the way, you'll find a wealth of resources, such as inspiring articles and platforms to kickstart your journey, plus an additional bonus of 100 more side hustles to explore.

It's important to note that this isn't a get-rich-quick scheme. Instead, consider it a guide to building sustainable, enjoyable side hustles that can grow with you over time. We're aiming for steady progress and long-term success, not overnight millions. The goal is to help you create additional income streams that align with your interests and skills, all while leveraging the power of AI to make the process more efficient and effective. If you want to replace your income, that is an option, too! Either way, it should spark ideas that can change your life.

This book offers a roadmap to potential financial freedom, enhanced by the power of AI. We'll combine innovative technology with your unique skills and interests to create opportunities that weren't possible just a few years ago. It's an exciting time to be an entrepreneur, and AI is opening doors to new possibilities every day.

The Structure of This Book

In this book, we will explore AI-powered side hustles in depth. We will cover the practical aspects of 'what' and 'how' you need to get started. Additionally, we will delve into the 'why' – the motivation behind pursuing these opportunities – and the 'what if' – the potential outcomes and possibilities they could lead to. Here's what you can expect:

- **Mindset for Success:** We'll discuss the entrepreneurial mindset needed to succeed with AI-powered side hustles. This includes tips on staying focused, managing your time, and continuously learning and adapting.
- **Understanding AI Tools:** We'll introduce ChatGPT and Dall-E, explaining how they work and how to use them effectively and ethically.
- **Getting Started with AI-Powered Side Hustles:** A comprehensive guide on beginning your journey, including assessing your skills, choosing the right side hustle, and setting up your digital workspace.
- **101 AI-Powered Side Hustles:** The book's core, where we'll explore a wide range of side hustle ideas across various industries and skill sets. Each idea will come with practical tips on getting started and leveraging AI tools for maximum efficiency.
- **Bonus:** 100 More AI-Assisted Side Hustle Ideas at a Glance
- **Conclusion:** A recap of key strategies and encouragement to take action on your AI-powered side hustle journey.
- **Resources:** "Your AI Side Hustle Resource Hub" – A curated list of platforms, tools, and additional resources discussed throughout the book to support and inspire your side hustle endeavors. Also included are 101 helpful articles offering further inspiration and insight for each side hustle, ensuring you have the knowledge and tools needed for success.
- **Side Hustle Index:** All 101 side hustles, listed by side hustle number for quick reference.

The AI Advantage

One of the most significant advantages of using AI in your side hustles is the ability to scale your efforts. AI can help you produce high-quality work more quickly, allowing you to take on more projects or clients. It can also help you venture into areas where you might not have expertise by assisting with tasks like writing in different styles or creating visual content.

However, it's crucial to remember that AI is a tool, not a replacement for human creativity and judgment. Throughout this book, we'll emphasize how to use AI to enhance your skills and ideas, not to substitute for them.

Are You Ready?

So, are you ready to turn your spare time into a source of income? Are you prepared to explore the cutting edge of AI and entrepreneurship? This book is your first step on an exciting journey. We'll help you navigate the intersection of technology and entrepreneurship, showing you how to leverage AI to create, innovate, and generate income in ways that weren't possible before.

Embracing AI-powered side hustles isn't just about earning extra income – it's about harnessing the power of cutting-edge technology to unlock new opportunities. By leveraging AI, you're positioning yourself to stay ahead of the curve, making your side hustle more efficient, scalable, and rewarding.

Let's begin this journey into the world of AI side hustles. Your path to financial freedom starts here!

Chapter One
Mindset for Success - Your AI Side Hustle Journey Begins in Your Head

"Success is not final, failure is not fatal: It is the courage to continue that counts."

Winston Churchill

Embarking on your AI side hustle journey is an exciting adventure with limitless possibilities. But before we dive into the practical tools and strategies, let's talk about something even more important: your mindset. The right mentality can distinguish between giving up at the first hurdle or building a thriving business that transforms your life. Success in this space isn't just about leveraging AI; it's about embracing growth, staying adaptable, and persevering through challenges.

Focus on One Side Hustle at a Time

With AI opening so many doors, it's easy to feel overwhelmed by all the possibilities. You might be tempted to jump from one idea to another, hoping to catch lightning in a bottle. But spreading yourself too thin can lead to burnout and disappointment. True mastery comes when you focus your energy and attention on one side hustle that aligns with your skills and interests. By dedicating yourself to it, you'll develop expertise, refine your processes, and gain the confidence to succeed.

Why focus matters:

- Focusing on one thing allows you to develop deep expertise that sets you apart.
- It helps you refine your approach and create a smoother path to success.
- Mastery in one area builds momentum and confidence and opens doors to future ventures.

Focus doesn't limit you – it empowers you. Committing to one side hustle allows you to grow, evolve, and, most importantly, succeed.

Action step: Choose a side hustle that resonates with your passion and skills. Commit to giving it your full attention for at least 90 days. Let this be your gateway to deep expertise and lasting success.

Set Realistic Goals and Expectations

While AI has the potential to boost your productivity, it's important to remember that success doesn't happen overnight. Setting realistic goals keeps you motivated and focused, helping you avoid frustration along the way. Achievable goals also make it easier to track progress, turning small wins into stepping stones toward bigger victories.

Goal-setting tips:

- Use the SMART framework (Specific, Measurable, Achievable, Relevant, Time-bound) to set clear and realistic goals.
- Break larger goals into smaller, manageable tasks so each step feels doable.
- Celebrate your small wins along the way; these build confidence and momentum.

Success isn't a race; it's a marathon. With each small goal you achieve, you're moving closer to your bigger vision.

Action step: Set a realistic, achievable goal for your first month of using AI in your side hustle. Aim for a challenge that stretches you but is within reach.

Cultivate Adaptability and a Growth Mindset

The world of AI is evolving rapidly. What worked yesterday might not work tomorrow, and that's okay. Adapting, adjusting, and embracing change is vital to thriving in this dynamic environment. A growth mindset – the belief that your abilities can improve with effort and learning – will keep you moving forward, even when you face obstacles.

How to stay adaptable and embrace growth:

- Stay curious about AI developments and be willing to change your strategies as needed.
- Dedicate weekly time to experiment with AI tools and explore new ways to enhance your side hustle.
- When you encounter setbacks, see them as opportunities to learn and grow, not failures.

Change is not a threat – it's an opportunity. You permit yourself to evolve and improve daily by cultivating a growth mindset.

Action step: Set up Google Alerts for key terms related to AI and learn one new thing about AI every week. Let growth become part of your journey.

Develop a Problem-Solving Mindset

At the heart of every successful side hustle is the ability to solve a problem. Whether you're helping customers save time, gain knowledge, or achieve their goals, your business exists to make someone's life easier. The key is to train your mind to identify problems and think creatively about solutions.

How to develop a problem-solving mindset:

- Practice active listening to understand your audience's challenges. The better you understand their needs, the better your solutions.
- Ask "What if?" and "How might we?" to brainstorm innovative ways to tackle problems.
- Look for inefficiencies or pain points in everyday processes, and think about how AI can create a smoother experience.

Every challenge is an invitation to innovate. By focusing on solutions, you're not just building a business but creating impact.

Action step: Each week, identify one problem in your personal or professional life. Use AI tools like ChatGPT to brainstorm creative solutions. Let problem-solving become part of your DNA.

Balance AI with Creativity and Personal Touch

While AI is a game-changer for efficiency and automation, your creativity and human touch are what truly set you apart. Customers seek connection, authenticity, and a personal experience that AI alone can't deliver. You'll build a business that resonates with people by striking the right balance between leveraging AI for efficiency and infusing your unique perspective.

Why balance matters:

- Increased efficiency allows you to focus on what matters most – delivering quality and value.
- Stronger customer relationships are built through personalized engagement, not just automated responses.
- Your unique brand identity thrives when AI enhances your creativity, not replaces it.

AI is a tool, not the whole story. Your personal touch is what makes your side hustle unforgettable.

Action step: Use AI to generate ideas or handle repetitive tasks for your next project. Then, take the time to refine and personalize the results with your creative input. Regularly review your content to ensure it reflects your unique vision.

Cultivate Financial Literacy

As your side hustle grows, financial literacy becomes crucial to scaling your success. Understanding basic financial principles helps you make smarter decisions about pricing, investments, and growth opportunities. Financial literacy gives you the clarity to manage your resources effectively and build a sustainable, profitable business.

Key financial concepts to understand:

- Profit margins and break-even points to ensure your side hustle is financially viable.
- Cash flow management, so you can plan for future growth without hitting roadblocks.
- Tax implications of running a side hustle, which will help you avoid surprises later.

Financial knowledge is power. Understanding the numbers behind your hustle gives you the tools to make decisions that fuel growth and sustainability.

Action step: Create a simple financial model for your side hustle, tracking projected income, expenses, and profits for the next six months. A free template is available in "Your AI Side Hustle Resource Hub" to help you get started.

Embrace Continuous Learning and Cultivate a Growth Mindset

In a world driven by AI, the ability to learn and adapt is your greatest asset. Success isn't just about mastering today's tools; it's about staying committed to growth, evolution, and curiosity. The most successful entrepreneurs understand that every challenge, every knowledge gap, is an opportunity to improve and innovate.

Why continuous learning matters:

- Overcoming knowledge gaps allows you to strengthen your skill set.
- Staying adaptable ensures you remain competitive as AI tools and trends change rapidly.
- Continuously improving your processes helps you increase efficiency and scale your business.

How to embrace the learning process:

- Dedicate time each week to experiment with AI tools and improve your skills.
- Identify areas where you need to grow and seek resources like courses, books, or mentors.
- Apply new knowledge immediately, reinforcing learning through action. Remember, every effort, including mistakes, contributes to mastery.

Learning isn't just an obligation – it's a privilege. With each new piece of knowledge, you're one step closer to mastering your side hustle.

Action step: Choose one aspect of your side hustle or AI tools you're less familiar with and dive in this week. Use resources like books, courses, or tutorials to strengthen your expertise, and apply what you learn right away.

Your Mindset is Your Superpower

As we wrap up this chapter, remember that your attitude and approach are as important as your skills and tools. Embrace focus, adaptability, creativity, and continuous learning as your guiding principles. Approach challenges with curiosity, set realistic goals, and always keep your customers in mind. With the right mindset, success is inevitable. You've already taken the first step by embarking on this journey – now it's time to fully commit and unlock your potential.

The world of AI-powered side hustles is waiting for you. Are you ready to seize the opportunity?

Chapter Two

Understanding AI Tools - Your New Digital Assistants

"The best way to predict the future is to create it."

Abraham Lincoln

As we embark on your AI-powered side hustle journey, it's important to understand the tools at your disposal. ChatGPT and Dall-E are two powerful AI systems that can revolutionize the way we work. This chapter will explore how to use these tools effectively, their capabilities, and how to maximize their potential in your side hustle.

Overview of ChatGPT and Dall-E

ChatGPT is a large language model designed to generate human-like text. It excels at understanding context, generating coherent responses, and helping with tasks like writing, brainstorming, and coding.

Dall-E creates unique, realistic images based on textual descriptions. It combines visual creativity with your written input, opening the door for custom visuals, logos, product designs, and more.

These tools offer a dynamic combination for content creation, marketing, and brand development.

For a deep dive into ChatGPT, check out our other book, "Unleashing the Millionaire Power of ChatGPT."

Crafting Effective AI Prompts

Crafting prompts is a vital skill when working with both ChatGPT and Dall-E. The more precise and thoughtful your prompts are, the better the output will be.

General Tips for Crafting Prompts:

- **Be clear and specific:** The AI needs details to understand your request.
- **Provide context:** Whether you're asking for an image or a blog post, provide background information to help the AI meet your expectations.
- **Iterate and refine:** Don't settle for the first result. Tweak the prompt, add specifics, and refine the output until it meets your vision.

Example Sequence for Prompt Refinement (ChatGPT):

- **Initial Prompt:** "Write a 300-word blog post about the benefits of using AI in side hustles."
- **Refine for Details:** "Expand the blog post to 500 words and focus on how ChatGPT can streamline content creation."
- **Expand for Examples:** "Include three examples of how ChatGPT can assist with content creation and add actionable tips."
- **Adjust Tone:** "Make the tone more conversational and break the post into smaller paragraphs for better readability."
- **Final Touches:** "Proofread the blog post and add a call-to-action at the end."

Example Sequence for Prompt Refinement (Dall-E):

- **Initial Prompt:** "Generate an image of a futuristic office chair."
- **Add Details:** "Make the chair ergonomic with a sleek, modern design and a metallic finish."
- **Specify Style and Mood:** "Set the chair in a minimalist environment with a clean, white background and soft, natural lighting to highlight the metallic elements."
- **Refine for Specificity:** "Adjust the perspective so the chair is at a slight angle, and add a small digital interface on the armrest for smart controls."
- **Final Touches:** "Enhance the metallic texture to make it look more reflective and adjust lighting for a slightly warmer tone."

ChatGPT: "Here is the image of the futuristic office chair based on the prompt refinement you provided!"

Using ChatGPT and Dall-E in Your Workflow

ChatGPT and Dall-E can streamline various aspects of your workflow, from content creation to visual design. Here's how to integrate them into your side hustle:

Content Creation with ChatGPT:

- **Blog posts:** "Write a blog post explaining the top 5 AI tools for entrepreneurs."
- **Product descriptions:** "Create a compelling product description for a smart water bottle that syncs with fitness apps."
- **Social media content:** "Generate five Twitter posts highlighting the importance of cybersecurity for small businesses."

ChatGPT will provide the written backbone for your projects, allowing you to focus on refining and personalizing the content.

Visual Design with Dall-E:

- **Book cover designs:** "Create a science fiction image set in a futuristic underwater city."
- **Product visualization:** "Generate an image of a sleek, ergonomic office chair designed for better posture."
- **Brand mascot creation:** "Design a cartoon-style robot mascot for a tech education company."

Dall-E transforms your written descriptions into compelling visuals, whether for product designs, marketing materials, or personal branding.

Practical Examples: AI Tools in Action

Let's explore specific examples of how ChatGPT and Dall-E can work together to supercharge your side hustle:

Example 1: Social Media Strategy

- **ChatGPT Prompt:** "Generate 5 engaging Instagram captions that promote sustainable living practices."
- **Dall-E Prompt:** "Create an image of a modern home with solar panels, surrounded by greenery, promoting sustainability."

Use these tools together to create compelling social media posts with engaging captions and custom visuals that resonate with your audience.

Example 2: Product Launch

- **ChatGPT Prompt:** "Write an email announcement for the launch of a new ergonomic office chair designed for home offices."
- **Dall-E Prompt:** "Generate a high-quality image of an ergonomic office chair with a modern design in a home office setting."

This combination allows you to create the email copy and the accompanying imagery for a professional product launch.

Example 3: Personal Branding

- **ChatGPT Prompt:** "Write a personal brand statement for a freelance graphic designer specializing in minimalist design."
- **Dall-E Prompt:** "Design a minimalist logo for a freelance graphic designer, using a simple monogram and neutral tones."

Pair ChatGPT's text generation capabilities with Dall-E's visual outputs to create a cohesive personal brand.

Ethical Use of AI Tools

Using AI tools responsibly is vital to maintaining authenticity and trust. As powerful as ChatGPT and Dall-E are, it's essential to maintain transparency about AI's role in your work.

- **Disclose AI assistance:** Whether you're using AI for content or images, be open about its involvement in your work.
- **Respect copyright and ownership:** Understand the limitations around AI-generated content and be cautious regarding intellectual property.
- **Avoid harmful content:** Be mindful of potential biases and always aim to create positive, ethical outputs.
- **Maintain your unique voice:** Use AI to enhance your work, not replace your personal input and creativity.

Troubleshooting Common Issues

As you work with ChatGPT and Dall-E, you may encounter challenges. Here's how to address some common issues:

- **Inconsistent outputs:** If ChatGPT gives different answers to the same question, refine your prompt for more consistency. For example: "You are a social media marketing expert. Please provide advice on improving engagement, ensuring it aligns with your previous responses."
- **Outdated information:** ChatGPT may provide outdated information. Always verify facts from up-to-date, reliable sources.
- **Unclear image outputs:** If Dall-E produces unclear or inaccurate images, provide more specific details about the

style, color, or mood you're aiming for in your prompt. Example: Instead of "a dog," try "a golden retriever puppy playing in a sunny park, painted in watercolor style."

Staying Ahead in the AI Landscape

AI is evolving rapidly, and staying informed is critical to success. To remain competitive and make the most of ChatGPT and Dall-E:

- **Follow AI news sources:** Subscribe to AI-focused newsletters to stay updated on the latest advancements. A list of newsletters is provided in "Your AI Side Hustle Resource Hub" at the end of the book.
- **Participate in AI communities:** Join forums or attend AI-related events to learn from others.
- **Experiment regularly:** Don't be afraid to try new tools or features as they become available. The more you experiment, the better you'll become at using AI to its fullest potential.

As we conclude this chapter, you should now understand ChatGPT and Dall-E, their capabilities, and how to integrate them into your workflow. These tools are incredibly powerful but truly shine when combined with your unique skills, experiences, and creativity. As you experiment with prompts, refine your outputs, and balance automation with personal input, you'll unlock new opportunities for growth and success in your side hustle.

In the following chapters, we'll explore specific side hustle ideas that leverage these AI tools. You'll see how the concepts discussed here can be applied to real-world business opportunities. Get ready to turn your AI knowledge into action and take your first steps towards AI-powered financial freedom!

Chapter Three
Getting Started with AI-Powered Side Hustles

"Success is the sum of small efforts, repeated day in and day out."

Robert Collier

Starting an AI-powered side hustle is an exciting opportunity to blend your passions, skills, and the cutting-edge capabilities of artificial intelligence. This chapter will guide you through each step, from assessing your skills to building your business, all while fueling your ambition to create something extraordinary. The key is to harness the transformative power of AI, align it with your unique talents, and take action toward building a fulfilling and profitable venture.

Discovering Your Skills and Passions

Before diving into any side hustle, especially one powered by AI, take a moment to reflect on your journey so far. What strengths have you developed? What passions fuel your energy? Aligning your venture with these will lead to a side hustle that doesn't just make money but ignites your creativity and satisfaction.

Identifying Your Strengths and Interests:

- **List your professional skills:** Write down the skills you've cultivated in your career – whether it's writing, marketing, design, or problem-solving.
- **Reflect on what excites you:** What activities make you lose track of time? What topics do you feel passionate about?
- **Seek external feedback:** Sometimes, we can't see our own strengths clearly. Ask trusted friends, family, or colleagues for their insights on what you do best.

The most rewarding side hustles align with your natural talents and passions. By building on what you're already good at and what you enjoy, you'll ensure that your hustle feels like an extension of who you are – not just another job.

Assessing Your AI Knowledge:

No matter where you are on your AI journey – beginner or advanced – this is the perfect time to take stock of your technical skills. You don't have to be an expert, but understanding where you stand will help you map out where to grow.

- **Evaluate your AI familiarity:** Are you comfortable with tools like ChatGPT or Dall-E? Do you know how to craft effective prompts? If not, it's time to embrace learning.
- **Identify skill gaps:** Don't be intimidated if AI is new to you. Look at this as an exciting opportunity to upskill. There are countless resources available to help you master AI fundamentals.
- **Learn as you go:** Don't wait until you're an expert to get started. Jump in and learn from every interaction you have with AI. The process of experimenting, making mistakes, and trying again will turn you into a master.

Choosing Your AI-Powered Side Hustle

Once you've discovered your strengths and identified areas for growth, it's time to select a side hustle that resonates with your unique blend of skills, passions, and the power of AI. This is where your creativity comes alive – where you find the intersection of what you're good at, what you love, and what the world needs.

Match Your Skills to Side Hustles:

The beauty of AI is that it can enhance virtually any skill set. Whether you're a writer, designer, marketer, or entrepreneur, there's an AI-powered side hustle waiting for you.

- **Content creators:** Use AI to streamline the writing process, generate ideas, and create high-quality content faster than ever.
- **Designers:** Leverage Dall-E for logo creation, product mockups, or unique illustrations that will set your designs apart.
- **Marketers:** Combine AI's ability to analyze data with your creativity to craft personalized marketing campaigns that resonate deeply with your audience.
- **The list goes on - there is something for everyone!**

Considering Time and Resources:

Dream big, but also be realistic about your time and resources. Your AI-powered side hustle should fit into your life, not overwhelm it.

- **Evaluate resources:** What tools or software will you need to get started? AI tools like ChatGPT and Dall-E offer incredible efficiency, but you may also need additional software or learning resources.
- **Balance learning with doing:** As you evaluate your time and resources, remember that every minute spent experimenting with AI is an investment in your future. Don't be afraid to learn on the job – action is often the best teacher.

Finding Your Niche:

Don't shy away from competition. Instead, find a niche that sets you apart. Consider how your unique background and experience can give you an edge. Combining your skills, interests, and AI tools can open up creative possibilities others haven't even considered.

- **Research market demand:** What services are people looking for? What problems can you solve more efficiently with AI?
- **Analyze the competition:** Look at what others are doing. What are they missing? How can you offer something unique by combining AI with your expertise?

Setting Up for Success: Your Digital Workspace

The environment you create for yourself profoundly impacts your productivity and success. Your workspace should be a reflection of your goals – organized, efficient, and inspiring.

Create a Productive Home Office:

Your workspace is more than just a physical place – it's where ideas turn into reality. Set up an environment that empowers you to focus and create.

- **Designate a dedicated area:** Even if it's just a corner of your living space, make it a place where you can focus on your side hustle.
- **Invest in the essentials:** A reliable computer and high-speed internet are critical for any AI-powered side hustle. Ensure your setup is ergonomic and comfortable.
- **Minimize distractions:** Remove clutter and distractions from your workspace. The clearer your space, the clearer your mind.

Ensure Data Security:

In today's digital world, data security isn't optional – it's essential. Safeguard your work and your client's information by implementing basic cybersecurity measures.

- **Invest in a secure connection:** High-speed, stable internet is important, but security is even more crucial. Consider using a VPN to protect your data.
- **Back up your work:** Use cloud storage to ensure that no matter what happens, your hard work is safe and accessible from anywhere.

Developing a Winning Business Plan

A business plan is your roadmap to success. It helps you define your goals, understand your market, and outline the steps you need to take to achieve them.

Define Your Services and Target Market:

Clarity is key when defining the services you offer and the clients you want to serve. Your business should be laser-focused on delivering value that AI can enhance.

- **Outline your services:** What will you offer, and how will AI improve those services? Be specific about what sets you apart from others in your industry.
- **Identify your ideal client:** Who are you trying to help? The more clearly you define your target market, the easier it will be to tailor your marketing and services to meet their needs.

Set Ambitious Yet Achievable Goals:

Success doesn't happen overnight, but with clear, measurable goals, you'll keep moving forward, step by step. Dream big, but break down your dreams into actionable steps.

- **Set short-term goals:** What do you want to achieve in your first 30, 60, or 90 days? These goals should be specific and measurable – whether it's landing your first client or mastering a new AI tool.
- **Set long-term goals:** Look ahead to six months and a year. What milestones will indicate success? These might include income targets, client satisfaction scores, or new skills you've learned.

Building Your Online Presence

In the digital age, your online presence is your storefront. It's how clients find, connect, and trust you.

Create a Professional Website:

Your website should be a reflection of your professionalism and creativity. It's where potential clients come to learn about what you offer and how AI enhances your services.

- **Design a clean, user-friendly site:** Ensure visitors can easily navigate and find information about your services.
- **Showcase your AI-powered skills:** Use case studies, before-and-after examples, and client testimonials to highlight how AI boosts your services.

Leverage Social Media:

Social media is a powerful tool for connecting with potential clients and sharing your expertise.

- **Choose the right platforms:** Focus on platforms where your target audience spends the most time.
- **Engage with your audience:** Post regularly and respond to comments to build a community around your services.

Pricing Your AI-Enhanced Services

Determining the right pricing for your services is both an art and a science. Your pricing strategy should reflect the value you bring, especially with the added efficiency and quality AI provides.

Factor in AI's Value:

AI enables you to work more efficiently, deliver higher-quality work, and scale your services. This added value should be reflected in your pricing.

- **Highlight AI's benefits:** When discussing pricing with clients, emphasize AI's benefits – faster turnaround times, improved quality, or more personalized results.

Managing Your Time and Scaling Responsibly

Your side hustle should fuel your ambition, not overwhelm you. Effectively managing your time and responsibly growing your business will guarantee long-term success and sustainability.

Time Management and Boundaries:

Setting clear boundaries and managing your time effectively is crucial to maintaining balance.

- **Set precise work hours:** Decide when you'll work on your side hustle and communicate these hours to your clients and loved ones.

- **Use productivity tools:** Apps like Trello, Notion, or time trackers can help you stay on track and organized.

Measuring Success and Iterating

Success is not a destination – it's a journey. Your AI-powered side hustle will evolve, and your ability to measure progress and make adjustments along the way will ensure long-term success.

Define Your Success Metrics:

The only way to know if you're succeeding is to define what success looks like. This could be income goals, client satisfaction, or personal fulfillment.

- **Track your KPIs:** Measure income, client retention, efficiency improvements, and personal growth. Regularly review these metrics and adjust your strategies accordingly.

- **Gather feedback:** After every project, seek feedback from your clients. Continuous improvement is the key to sustaining your success.

Your AI-Powered Journey Begins Now

You've laid the foundation, and now it's time to take action. The beauty of an AI-powered side hustle is that the possibilities are vast and varied. As you move forward, remember that success doesn't come from working harder but from working smarter – leveraging AI to amplify your skills and creativity.

You are ready to step into the world of AI-powered side hustles, where human ingenuity meets machine efficiency. With the guidance you've gained from this chapter, you can now confidently build a business that reflects your strengths, passions, and AI expertise.

Chapter Four
101 AI-Powered Side Hustles - Your Gateway to Financial Freedom

"The path to success is to take massive, determined action."

Tony Robbins

Welcome to the heart of your journey – a comprehensive exploration of 101 AI-powered side hustles that have the potential to transform your financial future. In the following sections, we'll dive into a wide array of opportunities, each harnessing the power of AI tools like ChatGPT and Dall-E to boost your productivity, spark creativity, and create new income streams.

These side hustles span industries and skill sets, from writing and design to marketing and education. Whether you're a creative professional seeking to diversify your income, a tech enthusiast eager to monetize your AI expertise, or someone entirely new to the side hustle world, you'll discover plenty of exciting possibilities here.

Each opportunity is designed to inspire, with some aligning perfectly with your strengths and others challenging you to explore new territory. This diversity is intentional – our talents, passions, and preferences shape the side hustles we're drawn to. To make your journey easier, we've included an index at the end of the book, listing each side hustle with its corresponding page number for quick reference.

As you explore these AI-powered opportunities, keep a journal to track the ideas that resonate with you. Inspiration often strikes when you least expect it. As you go through the book, new ideas for side hustles may come to mind. Jot them down and research them. Use ChatGPT to explore how you can succeed and what steps to take. Ask for platform suggestions and do your own internet searches. Look for successful people already doing it, and note how they got there. Watch YouTube videos, absorb as much as possible, and, most importantly, take action. Don't be discouraged by setbacks; remember to celebrate small wins along the way.

Consider Kevin, who started a simple dog-walking business. As his clientele grew, he built a website and hired other dog walkers to help. Along the way, he noticed many clients needed obedience training for their dogs, so he took a course, mastered the skill, and expanded his services. Kevin's business grew beyond what he initially imagined. Eventually, he even wrote a book on dog training!

Kevin's journey is a reminder that side hustles evolve. The opportunities you pursue today might open doors to entirely new ventures tomorrow. By journaling your thoughts and experiences, you'll capture insights that could lead to your next big idea.

As you progress, remember that success often comes from finding the sweet spot between your skills, passions, and market demand. Let's embark on this journey of discovery and see what possibilities await in the world of AI-assisted entrepreneurship.

What to Expect

For each side hustle, you'll find:

- A brief description of the opportunity
- Practical ways to use ChatGPT or Dall-E
- Potential earnings
- Recommended platforms
- Quick-start steps to get you going
- Tips for success

These side hustles are meant to serve as a starting point – stepping stones to ignite your entrepreneurial spark. Once you find a side hustle that resonates with you, we encourage you to dig deeper:

- Conduct thorough research on the industry and market demand
- Revisit the mindset tips in Chapter 1 to help you stay focused and motivated
- Connect with professionals who are already thriving in the field
- Watch tutorials and deep-dive videos on platforms like YouTube
- Join relevant online communities to share experiences and learn from others
- Stay updated on industry trends and emerging best practices

Remember: AI is an Enhancement, Not a Replacement

The true power of these AI-powered side hustles lies in using AI to amplify your creativity and skills – not to replace them. As you explore these opportunities, consider how each aligns with your goals and strengths. Your unique perspective, combined with AI tools, will set you apart in this ever-evolving digital landscape.

Your journey doesn't end with choosing a side hustle – it's just beginning. Success in this space is built on continuous learning, adapting to change, and persevering through challenges. Stay curious, embrace the learning process, and let AI be your tool for growth and innovation.

Are you ready to unlock your next AI-powered income stream? Let's dive in and discover the exciting potential that awaits!

Writing & Content Creation Side Hustles

The art of writing is the art of discovering what you believe."

Gustave Flaubert

In today's digital landscape, writing and content creation offer limitless side hustle opportunities, from blogging and e-books to copywriting and articles. AI tools like ChatGPT can act as a catalyst for creativity and productivity, helping you brainstorm ideas, generate outlines, and refine your writing process. This section explores how you can blend your natural writing talent with AI to streamline content creation and deliver engaging, high-quality work more efficiently. With AI enhancing your workflow, you'll have more time to focus on what truly matters – expressing your unique voice and building a profitable writing side hustle. Let AI assist, but remember, your passion for writing will leave a lasting impact.

1. Blog Writing

Do you love to write? Imagine turning your passion for words into a profitable side hustle, all while using AI to turbocharge your creativity! Blog writing allows you to craft engaging content on topics you're passionate about, and with the help of ChatGPT, you can brainstorm ideas, outline posts, and draft articles in record time. This means more writing time, more clients to serve, and more opportunities to grow your online presence!

Blog writing can complement many other side hustles. For example, if you write a book, you could create an author website and add a blog to keep your followers informed and engaged. You can also use a blog to promote other services, like freelance work or coaching. Add this idea to your notebook and consider how blog writing could enhance other side hustle ideas you pursue!

How to Use ChatGPT:

- **Idea Generation:** Brainstorm fresh and exciting topics.
- **Outline Creation:** Organize your thoughts with clear, concise outlines.
- **Drafting Content:** Get that first draft flowing faster than ever.
- **Expanding Key Points:** Add depth and detail with AI-driven insights.
- **Proofreading and Refining:** Polish your content to perfection.

Potential Earnings:

- $500-$2,000 per month, depending on the type of blog, traffic, and subscribers.

Platforms to Use:

- **Medium:** Reach a broad audience with ease.
- **WordPress:** Own your space with a custom blog.
- **Wix or other website builders:** Create a professional blog with user-friendly tools.
- **Freelance Marketplaces:** Pitch your writing services on **Upwork** or **Fiverr**.

Quick-Start Steps:

1. **Focus on What Drives You:** Choose a niche or topic you're enthusiastic about.
2. **Build Your Platform:** Set up your blog or create profiles on freelance platforms.
3. **Let AI Kickstart Your Creativity:** Use ChatGPT to brainstorm and draft your first few posts.
4. **Get the Word Out:** Promote your blog or pitch to potential clients.

Tips for Success:

- **Fact-Check and Personalize:** AI gives you the tools, but it's your job to ensure accuracy and infuse your unique voice.
- **Develop Your Voice:** Stand out by blending AI with your personal insights, experiences, and flair.
- **Be Consistent:** Regular posting builds credibility, grows your audience, and attracts clients.

ChatGPT can speed up the writing process, but your passion and personal touch will truly make your blog shine. Use AI to amplify your productivity, but let your creativity take center stage. After all, your unique voice is the heartbeat of every post, which will keep readers coming back for more!

2. E-book Writing

Do you have a wealth of knowledge or passion about a particular topic? Why not turn that into an income-generating e-book? E-book writing lets you dive deep into niche topics and share your expertise with the world, all while using ChatGPT to help you craft, organize, and refine your ideas faster than ever. Whether you're writing about personal development, DIY projects, or industry insights, e-books offer an incredible platform to showcase your knowledge and create a steady stream of passive income.

Remember, you can create an e-book for almost any side hustle! So, as you explore the different opportunities in this book, add this idea to your journal to expand on any other side hustle. It's a versatile option that fits virtually any industry, helping you reach a wider audience and boost your income.

How to Use ChatGPT:

- **Brainstorm E-book Topics:** Tap into AI's creativity to discover in-demand ideas.
- **Create Detailed Outlines:** Organize your chapters with clarity and structure.
- **Generate Chapter Summaries & Key Points:** Flesh out the core of each chapter.
- **Assist in Writing:** Have ChatGPT help with drafting individual sections or chapters.
- **Editing & Proofreading:** Use AI to refine your writing and ensure your e-book is polished.

Potential Earnings:

- $1000+ per month, depending on length, niche, and marketing efforts.

Platforms to Use:

- **Amazon Kindle Direct Publishing:** Reach millions of readers worldwide.
- **IngramSpark:** Expand your distribution to bookstores and libraries.

Quick-Start Steps:

1. **Choose Your Topic:** Choose a topic you're interested in that also has strong market demand.
2. **Create an Outline:** Use ChatGPT to create a detailed outline and compelling chapter summaries.
3. **Write Your E-Book:** Write your e-book using ChatGPT to assist you in generating content quickly and efficiently.
4. **Edit and Publish:** Edit, proofread, and format your e-book for publication on the platform of your choice.

Tips for Success:

- **Offer Unique Value:** Your e-book should go beyond what's freely available online – make sure it offers fresh insights, solutions, or strategies.
- **Personalize Your Content:** ChatGPT is a great assistant, but your personal expertise and experiences will make the content stand out.
- **Invest in Presentation:** Don't underestimate the power of a professional cover and compelling book description to attract readers.

E-book writing is more than just a side hustle; it's a way to establish your authority in a niche, all while generating income passively. ChatGPT can turbocharge your process, helping you turn ideas into fully fleshed-out books in less time. Get ready to see your name in digital print and start earning from your knowledge today!

3. Article Writing

Do you love researching, writing, and sharing your insights? Article writing offers a fantastic opportunity to express creativity, build authority in your niche, and generate a steady income. Whether you're writing for online publications, businesses, or blogs, ChatGPT can help you streamline the entire process – from brainstorming ideas to refining the final draft. With AI, you can increase your writing output and take on more clients without sacrificing quality.

How to Use ChatGPT:

- **Research and Gather Key Points:** Let ChatGPT assist you in compiling the essential facts and data for your topic.
- **Generate Article Outlines:** Structure your articles with a clear and logical flow.
- **Draft Introductions and Conclusions:** Create attention-grabbing openings and powerful wrap-ups.
- **Expand on Main Ideas:** Add depth and detail with examples, research, and well-crafted arguments.
- **Proofread and Edit:** With AI-driven editing assistance, ensure your articles are polished and error-free.

Potential Earnings:

- $300 to $1,000+ per article, depending on length, complexity, and the publication's prestige.

Platforms to Use:

- Fiverr: Find clients looking for a wide range of article writing services.
- Upwork: Build a portfolio and connect with clients globally.
- Contently: Gain access to top-tier publications and freelance gigs.
- **Wix or Other Website Builders:** Showcase your own blog or writing portfolio.

Quick-Start Steps:

1. **Identify Your Expertise:** Determine your areas of expertise or topics you enjoy writing about.
2. **Set Up Your Profiles:** Create profiles on freelance platforms or pitch directly to publication.
3. **Leverage ChatGPT for Writing:** Use ChatGPT to help with research, outlines, and drafting your first few articles.
4. **Build Your Portfolio:** Build a portfolio of published work to attract higher-paying clients.

Tips for Success:

- **Always Verify Facts:** ChatGPT is a great tool, but fact-check all information to ensure accuracy.
- **Develop Your Style:** Cultivate a unique writing voice that differentiates you from AI-only content.
- **Stay Updated:** Keep on top of current events and trends within your niches to offer timely, relevant content.

Article writing allows you to blend creativity and knowledge, and ChatGPT can help you maximize productivity. Hone your craft, grow your portfolio, and elevate your content writing side hustle with the perfect mix of human touch and AI efficiency!

4. Copywriting

Do you have a way with words and a knack for persuasion? Copywriting could be your ticket to transforming products, services, and brands with the power of compelling text. Whether you're crafting slogans, product descriptions, or entire marketing campaigns, ChatGPT can be your creative partner, helping you generate ideas and refine your copy faster than ever. The best part? This skill is in high demand across virtually every industry, offering unlimited opportunities to expand your client base and boost your earnings.

How to Use ChatGPT:

- **Brainstorm Catchy Slogans and Taglines:** Use AI to help spark memorable phrases that capture attention.
- **Generate Multiple Versions of Ad Copy for A/B Testing:** Rapidly produce variations to find the most effective messaging.
- **Draft Product Descriptions:** Highlight critical features and benefits, making products irresistible to customers.
- **Create Compelling Calls-to-Action (CTAs):** Drive conversions with clear, action-oriented language.

Potential Earnings:

- $40 - $120+ per hour, or project-based fees ranging from $100 - $1000+, depending on the scope and your experience.

Platforms to Use:

- **Freelancer:** Connect with a wide range of clients looking for expert copywriters.
- **Contently:** Join a network of high-quality freelancers working with top-tier brands.
- **Direct Client Acquisition:** Network, attend events, or build your website to attract clients.

Quick-Start Steps:

1. **Study Copywriting Techniques:** Study successful copywriting examples and techniques to understand what works.

2. **Build Your Portfolio:** Build a portfolio showcasing your copywriting skills (ChatGPT can help generate sample pieces).

3. **Market Your Services:** Set up profiles on freelance platforms or create your own website to market your services.

4. **Gain Experience:** Start with smaller projects to gain experience, collect testimonials, and build credibility.

Tips for Success:

- **Tailor ChatGPT's Output:** Always tailor ChatGPT's output to match the brand's voice and resonate with the target audience.

- **Understand Persuasion and Consumer Behavior:** Understand the psychology of persuasion and consumer behavior to create compelling, results-driven copy.

- **Test and Refine:** Continually test and refine your copy based on performance metrics to maximize impact.

Copywriting is all about influencing decisions and driving action. ChatGPT can provide a wealth of ideas and draft content quickly, but your expertise in refining that content to speak directly to the audience sets you apart. As you grow in this dynamic field, stay ahead by learning about marketing trends and consumer behavior to keep your copy fresh, relevant, and powerful. Using AI, you can elevate your copywriting game and create copy that stands out and converts.

5. Scriptwriting

Have you got a flair for storytelling? Scriptwriting could be your creative outlet, giving life to ideas through words that jump off the page and onto the screen. Whether you're writing for videos, podcasts, films, or presentations, ChatGPT can become your writing partner, helping you generate fresh ideas, develop characters, and refine dialogue. With AI speeding up the more repetitive tasks, you'll have more time to focus on crafting narratives that captivate audiences and tell powerful stories.

How to Use ChatGPT:

- **Brainstorm Plot Ideas and Character Concepts:** Quickly generate creative scenarios and characters to bring your story to fruition.

- **Generate Dialogue for Different Scenes:** Explore different dialogue options to fit your characters' personalities and the scene's mood.

- **Create Structured Outlines for Scripts:** Organize your ideas into a clear narrative flow that keeps the story engaging and on track.

- **Refine and Polish Dialogue or Narrative:** Use AI to clean up rough drafts, making your scripts sharper and more professional.

Potential Earnings:

- $30–$56 per hour of a finished script, or $500 - $5000+ per project, depending on the type, length, and experience.

Platforms to Use:

- **Fiverr:** Attract clients looking for scriptwriters across various media.
- **Upwork:** Offer your scriptwriting services to a broad range of clients, from startups to production companies.
- **Industry-specific job boards like Stage32:** Connect with film and media professionals looking for skilled scriptwriters.

Quick-Start Steps:

1. **Determine Your Niche:** Identify whether you want to focus on marketing videos, podcasts, short films, or other media types.
2. **Study Script Formats:** Learn about different storytelling techniques and script formats for your chosen area.
3. **Create Sample Scripts:** Use ChatGPT to assist you in creating polished examples for your portfolio.
4. **Build Your Presence:** Set up profiles on freelance platforms or pitch directly to production companies and clients.

Tips for Success:

- **Adapt ChatGPT's Output:** Adapt ChatGPT's output to suit the specific voice, tone, and style needed for each project.
- **Master Different Mediums:** Understand the intricacies of writing for various mediums, whether visual (video) or auditory (podcasts).
- **Improve Storytelling and Stay Current:** Continuously improve your storytelling skills and stay updated on trends within the entertainment and media industries.

ChatGPT can help with brainstorming and drafting, but the magic of scriptwriting comes from your creativity, ability to build tension, and skill in writing dialogue that sounds natural and authentic. As you refine AI-generated scripts, you'll create stories that resonate and engage audiences, from short films to branded content. Success in scriptwriting often comes from collaboration, so be open to feedback and revisions, building stronger narratives with every draft. With AI as your creative assistant, you'll be free to focus on what you do best – crafting stories that inspire, entertain, and move people.

6. Technical Writing

Imagine turning complex information into crystal-clear, accessible content that helps people understand cutting-edge products or processes. Does that sound like something you'd enjoy?! Well, that's the essence of technical writing –

transforming intricate details into simple, user-friendly documentation like user manuals, white papers, and product guides. With ChatGPT, you can streamline your writing process by organizing information, simplifying technical jargon, and ensuring consistency across even the most detailed documents.

How to Use ChatGPT:

- **Generate Outlines for Technical Documents:** Organize content logically to ensure clarity and flow.
- **Explain Complex Concepts:** Use AI to help translate complicated ideas into user-friendly language.
- **Create Step-by-Step Instructions:** Draft detailed procedures that are easy to follow, even for non-experts.
- **Draft Glossaries of Technical Terms:** Build clear definitions for industry-specific terms, enhancing reader comprehension.

Potential Earnings:

- $30 to $50+ per hour, or $500 - $5000+ per project, depending on complexity and your expertise.

Platforms to Use:

- **ClearVoice:** Find clients seeking specialized technical writing expertise.
- **Upwork:** Offer your skills to clients across various industries, from tech startups to established enterprises.
- **LinkedIn Jobs:** Explore full-time or freelance technical writing roles.
- **Mediabistro:** Discover opportunities in media, tech, and beyond.

Quick-Start Steps:

1. **Identify Your Expertise:** Determine which industries or technologies you know most or are interested in.
2. **Study Technical Writing Formats:** Familiarize yourself with common document formats like user manuals, white papers, or product guides.
3. **Create Sample Documents:** Use ChatGPT to help create polished technical writing samples for your portfolio.
4. **Build Your Online Presence:** Set up profiles on freelance platforms or apply for technical writing positions to start attracting clients.

Tips for Success:

- **Ensure Accuracy:** Always verify technical information ChatGPT provides with authoritative sources to maintain accuracy.

- **Hone Research Skills:** Develop strong research skills to grasp complex topics quickly and explain them effectively.
- **Master Essential Tools:** Learn industry-standard tools like **Adobe FrameMaker** or **MadCap Flare** for formatting and publishing.

Mastering the art of simplifying the complex can set you apart in the field of technical writing. Specializing in software, healthcare, or engineering industries can increase your market value, making you the go-to expert for clients needing crystal-clear documentation. Ready to dive in?

7. Social Media Content Creation

In the fast-paced world of social media, the power of captivating content can't be overstated. Imagine crafting engaging posts, writing scroll-stopping captions, and managing campaigns that captivate audiences and grow brands. If the idea of being at the heart of the digital conversation excites you, social media content creation is your ticket! With ChatGPT by your side, you can spark fresh ideas, develop content calendars, and compose high-impact posts – all with incredible efficiency. This enables you to juggle multiple clients or platforms while maintaining a consistent, high-quality presence online.

How to Use ChatGPT:

- **Generate Post Ideas:** Use AI to brainstorm content based on trending topics, brand messages, or product launches.
- **Craft Engaging Captions:** Let ChatGPT help you create compelling, on-brand captions that resonate with your audience.
- **Develop Hashtag Strategies:** Increase post visibility with targeted, research-backed hashtag strategies.
- **Draft Responses to Queries:** Streamline customer engagement by drafting thoughtful, personalized replies to common queries or comments.

Potential Earnings:

- $10 - $500+ per post, or $500 - $10,000+ per month for managing accounts, depending on the number of clients, platforms, and your expertise.

Platforms to Use:

- **Hootsuite**: Schedule posts, track performance, and manage multiple social media platforms in one place.
- **Buffer**: Simplify social media management with intuitive tools for scheduling, publishing, and analyzing content.
- **Freelance Marketplaces:** To reach a broad client base, offer your services on platforms like **Upwork** or **Fiverr**.

Quick-Start Steps:

1. **Master the Platforms:** Familiarize yourself with different social media platforms (**Instagram**, **Facebook**, **TikTok**,

LinkedIn) and their specific best practices

2. **Create a Sample Calendar:** Develop a sample content calendar for a hypothetical brand using ChatGPT for post ideas and captions.

3. **Set Up Your Profiles:** Build profiles on freelance platforms or reach out directly to local businesses to offer your social media management services.

4. **Diversify Your Content:** Use ChatGPT to help create various content types – captions, posts, stories, and even social media ads for your first clients.

Tips for Success:

- **Tailor AI Content:** Always adjust AI-generated content to reflect each brand's unique voice, tone, and style.
- **Stay Ahead of Trends:** Keep up with the latest social media trends and platform algorithm changes to ensure your content stays fresh and relevant.
- **Use Analytics:** Leverage data to fine-tune your content strategy and optimize engagement rates.

Social media content creation involves storytelling, relationship building, and consistently maintaining an engaging digital presence. ChatGPT can help you scale your content creation, but your unique understanding of audience behavior, platform trends, and brand strategy will set you apart. Keep refining your skills, specialize in key industries or platforms, and stay ahead by embracing the latest digital marketing trends. Your ability to deliver creative, effective social media strategies can open doors to a world of opportunities and clients.

8. SEO Content Writing

SEO content writing combines the art of crafting valuable, engaging content with the science of search engine optimization. Imagine writing content that captures your audience's attention and ranks high on Google, driving traffic to your client websites! With ChatGPT, you can quickly generate SEO-friendly content ideas, outline keyword-rich articles, and write posts that strike the perfect balance between readability and optimization. This allows you to efficiently create content that appeals to both search algorithms and human readers.

How to Use ChatGPT:

- **Generate Topic Ideas:** Use ChatGPT to discover content topics based on trending keywords or industry insights.
- **Craft Keyword-Rich Outlines:** Structure your content with outlines that naturally incorporate high-ranking keywords.
- **Write SEO-Optimized Meta Descriptions:** Let ChatGPT help you create compelling meta descriptions and title tags optimized for search engines.
- **Expand Key Points:** Use AI to develop relevant, keyword-rich content that keeps readers engaged while satisfying

search engine requirements.

Potential Earnings:

- $25 to $35 per hour or $1,000 - $10,000+ per month for ongoing work, depending on the volume, complexity, and your expertise.

Platforms to Use:

- **Textbroker:** Connect with clients seeking SEO content.
- **WriterAccess:** Join a platform dedicated to top-tier content creators.
- **Upwork:** Find a wide range of SEO writing gigs and build long-term partnerships.

Quick-Start Steps:

1. **Master SEO Basics:** Learn the essentials of SEO, including keyword research and on-page optimization.
2. **Use SEO Tools:** Familiarize yourself with tools like **Google Keyword Planner**, **SEMrush**, or **Ahrefs** to identify relevant keywords.
3. **Create a Portfolio:** Write a few sample SEO-optimized articles to showcase your skills.
4. **Pitch Clients:** Set up profiles on freelance platforms or reach out to digital marketing agencies with your portfolio.

Tips for Success:

- **Focus on the Reader:** While keywords are crucial, prioritize creating engaging, valuable content that speaks to human readers.
- **Stay Updated:** SEO is ever-evolving. Keep up with Google algorithm updates and SEO trends to maintain your edge.
- **Refine AI-Generated Content:** Use ChatGPT to get started, but always edit for originality, depth, and quality.

SEO content writing is where creativity meets strategy. By blending engaging storytelling with optimized keyword usage, you'll deliver content that ranks high in search results while offering real value to readers. As you master the nuances of SEO, you'll unlock high-earning potential and develop long-term client relationships. Keep learning, refining, and positioning yourself as an SEO expert who understands the power of words and algorithms!

9. Newsletter Creation

Are you excited about connecting people with valuable content? Newsletter creation is all about crafting engaging and informative content that keep subscribers hooked and coming back for more. Whether creating newsletters for businesses or building your own subscriber base, ChatGPT can help streamline the process – sparking fresh ideas, writing captivating subject lines, and producing polished content. With AI at your side, you'll be able to create newsletters that engage and drive results while managing more clients and expanding your reach.

Think about how a newsletter could amplify other side hustles you explore. Whether it's keeping clients updated on new services or sharing insights related to your niche, a well-designed newsletter can help you build deeper connections and keep your audience engaged. Don't forget to jot that into your notebook to expand your side hustle potential!

How to Use ChatGPT:

- **Brainstorm Newsletter Themes:** Tap into AI's creativity to discover timely and relevant topics.
- **Craft Attention-Grabbing Subject Lines:** Use ChatGPT to generate subject lines that boost open rates.
- **Draft Content Sections:** Get assistance writing introductions, feature articles, or subscriber updates.
- **Create Engaging Calls-to-Action (CTAs):** Draft CTAs encouraging readers to engage, click, and take action.

Potential Earnings:

- $10,000 in monthly revenue or $120,000 per year, depending on the number of subscribers and subscription cost.

Platforms to Use:

- **Substack:** Build your own paid newsletter and reach an engaged audience.
- **Mailchimp:** Manage newsletters for clients and grow their subscriber base.
- **Upwork** or **Fiverr:** Find freelance opportunities to offer your newsletter services to businesses.

Quick-Start Steps:

1. **Study Successful Newsletters:** Research newsletters in various industries to understand formats and strategies that work.
2. **Master Email Marketing Basics:** Learn segmentation, A/B testing, and other essential marketing tactics.
3. **Create Sample Newsletters:** Use ChatGPT to draft portfolio examples that showcase your ability to create engaging newsletters.
4. **Pitch Clients:** Set up profiles on freelance platforms or approach businesses directly, offering to help grow their email outreach.

Tips for Success:

- **Tailor Content:** Adjust AI-generated content to reflect the brand's unique voice and speak to the audience's needs.
- **Provide Value:** Don't just sell – create content that educates, entertains, or informs, offering true value to your subscribers.
- **Refine with Analytics:** Use open rates, click-through rates, and other metrics to improve your newsletter strategy continuously.

Newsletters are a powerful way to build relationships with an audience, but success hinges on delivering real value. ChatGPT can help you with the writing, but your role is to ensure each newsletter speaks directly to your readers, keeping them engaged and loyal. With the right strategy, you can turn newsletter creation into a lucrative, impactful side hustle that grows over time. Keep honing your email marketing skills and stay updated on trends to maximize the value you offer clients and subscribers.

10. Ghostwriting

Have you ever thought about using your writing skills to shape someone else's story or give their ideas a voice? Ghostwriting is all about crafting high-quality content – books, articles, speeches, or social media posts – published under another's name. With ChatGPT as your creative partner, you can brainstorm, outline, and draft content in a way that truly captures your client's voice, all while managing multiple projects more efficiently. This enables you to excel in a wide range of styles and mediums, boosting your productivity and expanding your client base.

How to Use ChatGPT:

- **Brainstorm Content Ideas:** Use AI to help generate topics or book ideas that align with your client's expertise.
- **Create Chapter Outlines or Article Structures:** Organize the content flow to ensure clear, engaging material.
- **Draft in the Client's Voice:** ChatGPT can assist with writing sections in a specific tone or style that matches the client's unique voice.
- **Refine & Polish:** Get help improving readability, clarity, and flow while maintaining the client's ideas.

Potential Earnings:

- $0.01 to $ 1+ per word for books, $100 - $500+ per article, or $20,000 up to $100,000+ per year, depending on the scope and your experience.

Platforms to Use:

- **Reedsy:** A platform connecting authors with professional ghostwriters.
- **The Urban Writers:** Find ghostwriting projects for books, articles, and more.
- **Freelance Platforms:** **Fiverr**, **Upwork**, and **Freelancer** are ideal for finding new clients.

- **LinkedIn:** Network with potential clients or literary agents and publishers directly.

Quick-Start Steps:

1. **Master Different Styles:** Practice writing in various genres and tones to broaden your skills.
2. **Create a Writing Portfolio:** Use ChatGPT to draft diverse writing samples showcasing your adaptability.
3. **Establish an Online Presence:** Set up profiles on freelance platforms or build a professional website to attract clients.
4. **Network with Clients & Agents:** Reach out to potential clients, publishers, or their representatives through online platforms.

Tips for Success:

- **Adapt to Various Styles:** Hone your ability to mimic different writing styles to match each client's voice.
- **Interview for Insights:** Develop strong interviewing skills to draw out important details and ensure authenticity in your writing.
- **Maintain Confidentiality:** Always respect client privacy and ensure contracts are clear on the scope of work and credit.

Ghostwriting is stepping into your client's shoes and conveying their thoughts, experiences, and expertise. ChatGPT can help streamline the writing process, but your ability to blend AI-generated content with personal interviews and research will make the writing distinguishable. Flexibility is key, as ghostwriting projects can vary widely. By mastering this skill and delivering high-quality, personalized content, you'll build a stellar reputation that leads to referrals and long-term clients. In this word-of-mouth industry, trust and excellence are everything!

11. Resume Writing

Imagine being the reason someone lands their dream job! Resume writing is crafting a professional, tailored resume and cover letter that sets your client apart from the competition. With ChatGPT, you can streamline the process by generating achievement-oriented bullet points, creating compelling professional summaries, and optimizing content for Applicant Tracking Systems (ATS). This allows you to efficiently help more job seekers, delivering resumes that stand out in today's competitive job market.

How to Use ChatGPT:

- **Generate Achievement-Focused Bullet Points:** Use AI to turn job descriptions into powerful, results-driven statements.
- **Create Tailored Summaries:** Draft objective statements or professional summaries highlighting the client's

strengths.

- **Craft Persuasive Cover Letters:** ChatGPT can help you create custom cover letters that reflect vital qualifications.
- **ATS Optimization:** Suggest industry-specific keywords to boost your client's chances of passing ATS filters.

Potential Earnings:

- $50 to $400 per resume, depending on the client's career level and your expertise.

Platforms to Use:

- **LinkedIn ProFinder:** Perfect for connecting with professionals who need resume services.
- **Indeed:** Leverage the platform to offer resume-writing services to job seekers.
- **Freelance Platforms: Fiverr, Upwork**, or even your own website for direct client acquisition.
- **Local Networking:** Attend job fairs and career coaching events or partner with recruiters to find clients.

Quick-Start Steps:

1. **Master Resume Trends:** Study current resume writing best practices and ATS requirements to deliver up-to-date formats.
2. **Create a Portfolio:** Build sample resumes for various industries and career levels to showcase your skills.
3. **Set Up Profiles:** Establish a presence on freelance platforms or build a professional website for your services.
4. **Network for Referrals:** Partner with career coaches, recruiters, or local job search groups to expand your client base.

Tips for Success:

- **Personalize Every Resume:** Always customize AI-generated content to reflect the client's unique experience and career goals accurately.
- **Stay Updated:** Keep up with industry trends and job market shifts to ensure your clients' resumes stay relevant.
- **Design Like a Pro:** Learn to use tools like Canva or Microsoft Word templates to create visually appealing resumes that stand out.

Resume writing is an advantageous way to help people advance their careers, and ChatGPT makes the process faster and more efficient. But your understanding of each client's story and job needs will make their resume shine. You can establish yourself as a go-to expert by specializing in specific industries or career levels and offering additional services like LinkedIn profile optimization or interview coaching. Build your reputation by delivering results, and watch as referrals and success come rolling in!

12. Grant Writing

Have you ever thought about being the person behind securing the funds that can transform communities, launch groundbreaking research, or fuel important social initiatives? That's the power of grant writing! This side hustle lets you use your writing and research skills to make a tangible difference by crafting compelling proposals for non-profits, research institutions, and more. By leveraging ChatGPT, you can streamline the process, structure persuasive proposals, and deliver high-quality submissions that stand out to funders, allowing you to tackle more projects and help more causes succeed.

How to Use ChatGPT:

- **Generate Outlines:** Develop detailed outlines to match the unique requirements of each grant.
- **Draft Project Descriptions:** Write clear, persuasive descriptions of the project's purpose and impact.
- **Craft Budget Justifications:** Develop budget narratives explaining how funds will be used.
- **Create Impact Statements:** Highlight the transformative outcomes of the project through powerful language.

Potential Earnings:

- $20 - $150+ per hour, depending on the complexity and your experience.

Platforms to Use:

- **GrantWriterTeam:** Collaborate with non-profits seeking funding expertise.
- **Upwork:** Offer your grant writing services to a wide range of organizations.
- **Non-Profit Job Boards (e.g., Idealist.org):** Connect with non-profits and research groups needing grant proposals.

Quick-Start Steps:

1. **Study Winning Proposals:** Analyze successful grant applications to understand funder expectations.
2. **Master the Basics:** Learn the essential elements of grant proposals, such as goals, budgets, and evaluations.
3. **Build a Portfolio:** Create sample grant proposals (label them as examples) to showcase your skills.
4. **Network with Non-Profits:** Reach out to local non-profits, research institutions, or educational programs that could benefit from your services.

Tips for Success:

- **Tailor Every Proposal:** Customize AI-generated content to align with specific funder goals and the organization's mission.
- **Research Funding Opportunities:** Master the art of finding the right grants for the right project.
- **Simplify Complex Ideas:** Use clear, engaging language to make complex concepts accessible to non-expert reviewers.

In grant writing, your work can help secure the resources needed to turn important projects into reality. ChatGPT can help you manage the process more efficiently, and your expertise in writing persuasive proposals will lead you to success. Specializing in specific fields or types of grants, building strong research skills, and staying on top of funder trends will elevate your side hustle. With each successful grant, you're not just delivering a proposal – you're changing lives, one project at a time.

13. Speech Writing

Have you ever thought about creating words that inspire crowds, stir emotions, or leave a lasting impact at a corporate event or wedding? That's the magic of speech writing! Whether it's for a CEO's keynote or a heartfelt wedding toast, you have the power to craft speeches that resonate with audiences and deliver powerful messages. With ChatGPT as your creative partner, you can streamline the brainstorming, structuring, and writing process, allowing you to take on more clients while producing polished, impactful speeches for every occasion.

How to Use ChatGPT:

- **Brainstorm Topics:** Generate speech topics and themes tailored to the speaker's needs and event.
- **Create Outlines:** Develop structured outlines with critical points, smooth transitions, and logical flow.
- **Craft Openings & Closings:** Write attention-grabbing introductions and memorable closings that stick with the audience.
- **Develop Anecdotes & Examples:** Create relatable anecdotes or vivid examples to illustrate the speaker's main points.

Potential Earnings:

- $35 - $350+ per hour, or $500 - $5,000+ per speech, depending on the length, complexity, and experience.

Platforms to Use:

- **Upwork:** Find clients looking for speech writing services.
- **Fiverr:** Offer quick-turnaround speeches for various events.

- **LinkedIn:** Network with corporate clients and professionals in need of personalized speeches.

Quick-Start Steps:

1. **Study Famous Speeches:** Analyze speeches from great orators to understand different structures and techniques.
2. **Practice Writing:** Use ChatGPT to help draft speeches for various occasions (weddings, corporate events, etc.).
3. **Build a Portfolio:** Create a portfolio with sample speeches that showcase your versatility and creativity.
4. **Set Up Profiles:** List your services on freelance platforms or create a website to promote your speech writing expertise.

Tips for Success:

- **Tailor to the Speaker's Voice:** Adapt AI-generated content to reflect the speaker's personality and delivery style.
- **Know the Audience:** Research the event and audience to ensure the speech resonates and is appropriate.
- **Master Verbal Flow:** Learn about verbal pacing and emphasis to structure speeches that sound great when delivered.

As a speech writer, your words have the power to move, motivate, and connect with people on a deep level. ChatGPT can help with the logistics, but your real value comes from crafting speeches that reflect the speaker's authentic voice and make an impact. By mastering speech structures and understanding audience dynamics, you'll become the go-to writer for everything from heartfelt wedding toasts to high-stakes business presentations. Specializing in specific speech types can open doors to working with high-profile clients and create lasting success in this inspiring side hustle.

14. Course Content Creation

Are you enthusiastic about teaching and love sharing your knowledge with others? Course content creation allows you to craft transformative educational experiences for online learners or in-person classes. From lesson plans to interactive quizzes, you'll create materials that help students grasp complex subjects and achieve their goals. Using ChatGPT, you can efficiently develop course outlines, draft engaging lesson content, and design assessments that resonate with learners of all styles. This enables you to streamline your workflow, producing top-tier educational resources faster than ever!

Course content creation can also be something you expand on with many of the other side hustle ideas in this book. As you explore different opportunities, consider how course creation could complement them. Add that to your journal and start brainstorming how to build educational components for each venture you pursue!

How to Use ChatGPT:

- **Generate Course Outlines:** Structure your course into modules that guide learners through progressively complex topics.

- **Draft Lesson Content:** Write clear explanations of key concepts and develop comprehensive lesson plans.
- **Create Discussion Prompts:** Develop thought-provoking questions and activities to engage students in deeper learning.
- **Develop Quiz Questions:** Create assessments that evaluate comprehension and retention of course material.

Potential Earnings:

- $1,000 to $10,000 per month, depending on the length, how much you charge, complexity, and your expertise.

Platforms to Use:

- **Teachable:** Build and sell your own courses online.
- **Udemy:** Reach a global audience with your educational content.
- **Upwork:** Find clients needing course content tailored to their training needs.

Quick-Start Steps:

1. **Identify Your Expertise:** Pinpoint the subjects or topics you're interested in teaching.
2. **Learn Instructional Design:** Familiarize yourself with e-learning principles and the best practices for structuring effective courses.
3. **Create a Sample Course:** Design a mini-course using ChatGPT to assist with content creation and structuring.
4. **Pitch Your Skills:** Set up profiles on freelance platforms or reach out to educational institutions to showcase your portfolio.

Tips for Success:

- **Tailor Content for Learners:** Always customize AI-generated material to meet the course objectives and your students' needs.
- **Engage All Learning Styles:** Incorporate a mix of visual, auditory, and hands-on activities to cater to diverse learners.
- **Stay Ahead of Trends:** Keep up with the latest developments in educational technology and online learning platforms to enhance your course.

Course content creation is your gateway to impacting countless learners and helping them grow and succeed. ChatGPT can help you craft polished, dynamic content, but your passion for teaching and your ability to connect with learners will make your courses stand out. By combining AI with your educational expertise, you'll create valuable learning experiences and carve out a rewarding side hustle in education. Get ready to inspire, educate, and change lives – one course at a time!

15. Research Paper Writing

Do you love diving deep into topics and uncovering new insights? Research paper writing allows you to explore academic or scientific subjects, analyze findings, and contribute meaningful work to scholarly communities. With ChatGPT, you can streamline the research process, organize complex ideas into structured outlines, and easily draft high-quality sections. This lets you tackle more projects, broaden your expertise, and enhance your academic output – all while making a significant impact through your writing.

How to Use ChatGPT:

- **Generate Research Questions:** Use AI to brainstorm insightful research questions and craft hypotheses.
- **Create Paper Outlines:** Organize your paper with comprehensive outlines that guide your argument logically.
- **Summarize Existing Research:** Quickly paraphrase and summarize key findings from existing literature.
- **Draft Core Sections:** Write compelling introductions, detailed methodologies, and clear conclusions with ChatGPT's assistance.

Potential Earnings:

$25 to $40 per hour, depending on the complexity, length, and your expertise.

Platforms to Use:

- **Academia-Research:** A platform for academic and scientific writing gigs.
- **Upwork:** Connect with academic writing clients looking for expert-level research support.
- **Freelancer:** Showcase your skills to find research-based projects.

Quick-Start Steps:

1. **Master Academic Writing Styles:** Familiarize yourself with APA, MLA, and Chicago citation formats.
2. **Learn Research Tools:** Develop skills in using academic databases (Google Scholar, JSTOR) and citation management software.
3. **Create Sample Papers:** Build a portfolio of research papers in your expertise, using ChatGPT to assist with content generation.
4. **Network & Pitch:** Reach out to academic institutions or set up profiles on freelance platforms to connect with potential clients.

Tips for Success:

- **Fact-Check AI Outputs:** Always verify the accuracy of AI-generated content and fact-check findings for academic rigor.
- **Hone Your Analytical Skills:** Develop your ability to analyze sources and synthesize information into a coherent argument critically.
- **Stay Updated in Your Field:** Keep up with the latest developments in your area of research to ensure your work remains relevant and credible.

Research paper writing is a rewarding path for those who enjoy in-depth analysis and making meaningful contributions to scholarly knowledge. With ChatGPT, you can optimize the more labor-intensive aspects of the writing process, allowing you to focus on delivering insightful, original work. Whether you specialize in scientific research, social sciences, or humanities, this side hustle will enable you to impact the academic world while growing your expertise. Embrace the power of AI to boost your productivity while maintaining the integrity and intellectual depth that makes your work stand out. Ready to dive into a world of research and discovery?

16. Podcast Writing

Do you have a passion for storytelling and love the art of conversation? Podcast writing allows you to create engaging, structured content that resonates with audiences through the power of audio. With ChatGPT, you can effortlessly brainstorm episode ideas, develop cohesive show outlines, and craft captivating scripts that match the podcast's unique tone. This enables you to produce consistent, high-quality episodes, helping you meet tight deadlines while maintaining creativity and originality.

How to Use ChatGPT:

- **Brainstorm Episode Topics:** Use AI to generate fresh, relevant themes and topics based on your podcast's niche.
- **Create Episode Outlines:** Structure your episodes with key talking points to ensure smooth transitions and flow.
- **Draft Introductions & Segues:** Compose compelling openings, transitions, and conclusions that keep listeners engaged from start to finish.
- **Generate Interview Questions:** Craft insightful, thought-provoking questions for guest episodes to spark meaningful conversations.

Potential Earnings:

- $25 - $100+ per hour, depending on your expertise.

Platforms to Use:

- **Podbean:** A platform for launching, promoting, and monetizing podcasts.

- **Fiverr:** Offer your podcast writing services to a wide range of clients.
- **Upwork:** Connect with podcasters who need expert scriptwriters and content creators.

Quick-Start Steps:

- **Study Popular Podcasts:** Analyze different genres and styles to understand what makes podcast scripts engaging.
- **Learn Audio Storytelling:** Familiarize yourself with audio production techniques and storytelling principles that resonate in a podcast format.
- **Create Sample Scripts:** Develop sample episodes using ChatGPT to assist with ideas and content generation.
- **Build Your Presence:** Set up profiles on freelance platforms or reach out directly to podcast producers to offer your services.

Tips for Success:

- **Adapt Content to the Podcast's Voice:** Ensure AI-generated scripts align with the podcast's brand, tone, and style for a seamless listener experience.
- **Master Audio Pacing:** Develop a keen understanding of timing, pacing, and how to maintain listener engagement in an audio format.
- **Stay Current:** Keep up with trends, events, and topics relevant to the podcast's niche to ensure timely and engaging content.

Podcast writing is creating an immersive audio experience that captivates and informs listeners. ChatGPT can help you generate ideas and structure scripts, but your creativity and ability to connect with the audience make the magic happen. Specialize in particular podcast genres, develop your skills in sound design, and network with podcasters to grow your client base. Whether crafting a solo show or writing for a panel discussion, this side hustle has endless possibilities. Ready to help podcasts reach new heights?

17. Press Release Writing

Are you excited about helping companies and organizations get their big announcements into the world? Press release writing is crafting concise, newsworthy statements that capture media attention and amplify a brand's message. With ChatGPT, you can brainstorm fresh angles, craft compelling headlines, and produce polished press releases that resonate with journalists and target audiences. This AI-enhanced approach allows you to create press releases quickly and effectively, helping companies get their stories in front of the right people faster than ever!

How to Use ChatGPT:

- **Brainstorm Newsworthy Angles:** Generate unique perspectives on company announcements to make them stand out.

- **Create Catchy Headlines & Subheadings:** Use AI to craft attention-grabbing headlines that draw in journalists and media outlets.
- **Draft Boilerplate Company Descriptions:** Quickly write clear, concise descriptions that capture the essence of the company or organization.
- **Compose Quotes from Company Representatives:** Create thoughtful, impactful quotes that add credibility and personality to the release.

Potential Earnings:

- $1 per word, or $500 for a 400-500 word press release, depending on the client, complexity, and your experience.

Platforms to Use:

- **PRWeb:** An online distribution service that helps businesses share their news with media outlets.
- **PR Newswire:** A trusted platform for distributing press releases across industries.
- **Upwork** & **Fiverr:** Connect with clients needing expert press release writers.

Quick-Start Steps:

1. **Study Successful Press Releases:** Familiarize yourself with industry-standard press release formats and journalism writing styles.
2. **Learn Press Release Structure & AP Guidelines:** Master the format and language journalists prefer to increase your chances of media coverage.
3. **Create Sample Press Releases:** Write releases for hypothetical company milestones to build a portfolio.
4. **Build Your Presence:** Set up profiles on freelance platforms or pitch your services directly to local businesses and organizations.

Tips for Success:

- **Fact-Check All Information:** Ensure all details, quotes, and facts are accurate, even when using AI to generate content.
- **Develop a Newsworthy Sense:** Learn what makes a story media-worthy and how to frame company announcements to capture attention.
- **Network with Journalists & Media Contacts:** Build relationships with key media professionals to increase the chances of getting your press releases published.

Writing press releases requires understanding the media landscape and crafting content that informs, excites, and engages. ChatGPT can assist with content creation and organization, but the real magic happens when you combine AI-generated content with your media expertise. Specialize in industries that align with your strengths and hone your storytelling and media relations skills. You can carve out a niche as a go-to press release writer by creating compelling, newsworthy content that speaks to companies and journalists. Ready to help brands and businesses share their biggest news with the world?

18. Product Description Writing

Imagine transforming everyday products into must-have items with nothing but your words! Product description writing is crafting engaging, informative content highlighting a product's unique features and benefits, helping customers make confident purchase decisions. Whether you're writing for an e-commerce website, a catalog, or a marketplace, ChatGPT can help you generate creative, benefit-driven descriptions that grab attention and drive sales. This streamlines your writing process, allowing you to produce more high-quality descriptions and adapt easily to different product types and brand voices.

How to Use ChatGPT:

- **Generate Unique Angles:** Use AI to find fresh and creative ways to highlight a product's key features.
- **Create Benefit-Focused Bullet Points:** Quickly develop bullet points that list features and emphasize how they benefit the customer.
- **Craft Attention-Grabbing Opening Lines:** Start with a hook that piques customers' curiosity.
- **Develop Persuasive Calls-to-Action:** Write clear, compelling calls-to-action that encourage immediate purchases.

Potential Earnings:

$3 - $25+ per product description or $15 to $100 per hour, depending on the volume and complexity of products.

Platforms to Use:

- **Shopify:** Work directly with e-commerce store owners to optimize product listing.
- **Etsy:** Help sellers showcase handmade and vintage products with compelling descriptions.
- **Upwork** & **Fiverr:** Find clients across various industries looking for expert product description writers.

Quick-Start Steps:

1. **Study Successful Descriptions:** Research popular e-commerce platforms and take note of product descriptions that catch your attention.
2. **Learn E-commerce SEO:** Understand the basics of search engine optimization (SEO) for product listings to help your clients rank higher in searches.

3. **Build Your Portfolio:** Write sample product descriptions across different niches to showcase your versatility.

4. **Create Your Presence:** Set up profiles on freelance platforms or pitch directly to e-commerce businesses needing engaging product content.

Tips for Success:

- **Research Every Product Thoroughly:** Ensure that your descriptions are not only creative but also accurate and detailed.

- **Adapt to Each Brand's Voice:** Tailor your writing to match the brand's unique style and tone to ensure consistency across product listings.

- **Focus on Benefits Over Features:** Highlight how the product will improve the customer's life, not just what it does.

Creating product descriptions is more than listing features – it's about showing how a product will solve a problem or enhance a customer's lifestyle. ChatGPT can help you produce descriptions quickly, but your creativity and attention to detail will make each one stand out. To build expertise and a solid portfolio, consider specializing in specific industries or product categories. By staying updated on e-commerce trends, mastering SEO, and understanding consumer behavior, you can help businesses drive sales and elevate their online presence. The more you refine your skills, the more valuable you'll become to brands and companies!

19. Story Writing

Do you dream of crafting tales that transport readers to far-off lands, tug at their heartstrings, or leave them pondering life's biggest questions? Storywriting allows you to create immersive fictional worlds, memorable characters, and gripping plots. With ChatGPT as your writing companion, you can spark new ideas, craft character backstories, and draft compelling narratives. This AI-powered tool will streamline your creative process, helping you overcome writer's block and produce captivating stories more efficiently – all while keeping your creative flair at the forefront.

How to Use ChatGPT:

- **Brainstorm Unique Plot Concepts:** Generate fresh ideas and unexpected twists to keep your readers hooked.

- **Develop Character Profiles:** Craft deep, multi-dimensional characters with detailed backstories and motivations.

- **Create World-Building Elements:** Map out immersive fantasy worlds or futuristic sci-fi settings with ChatGPT's assistance.

- **Draft Dialogue:** Write engaging and realistic character exchanges that bring your story to life.

Potential Earnings:

Varies widely. $0.01 - $1+ per word for short stories, $1,000 - $10,000+ for novellas or novels, depending on publication method and your reputation.

Platforms to Use:

- **Wattpad:** Build an audience by publishing your work and gaining reader feedback.
- **Amazon Kindle Direct Publishing:** Self-publish your stories for global distribution and earn royalties.
- **Traditional Publishing Houses:** Pitch your completed manuscript to literary agents for potential book deals.

Quick-Start Steps:

1. **Hone Your Voice:** Develop a unique writing style that captures readers' imaginations.
2. **Create a Portfolio:** Write short stories or complete a novel to showcase your storytelling abilities.
3. **Get Published:** Start with platforms like Wattpad or query agents for traditional publishing opportunities.
4. **Build an Author Platform:** Connect with readers and other writers on social media to expand your fan base.

Tips for Success:

- **Infuse Creativity:** Use AI to spark ideas, but ensure your creative voice drives the story.
- **Refine Your Drafts:** Develop your editing skills to perfect AI-assisted drafts.
- **Join Writing Communities:** Engage with fellow writers for support, feedback, and networking opportunities.

Storytelling is an art form only you can master – no AI can replace the passion and creativity you bring to the page. ChatGPT can enhance your process, but your ideas, voice, and imagination will captivate readers. As you evolve in your writing side hustle, consider specializing in genres you're interested in, from fantasy to mystery to romance. Deepen your understanding of the publishing industry and connect with your readers to build a loyal audience. With persistence and creativity, you can transform storytelling into a fulfilling, successful side hustle – start crafting your next masterpiece today!

20. Proofreading

Proofreading could be your ideal side hustle if you enjoy perfecting the finer details. Proofreading is the process of improving grammar, style, clarity, and consistency in written content. While human judgment is crucial, tools like ChatGPT can enhance this process by suggesting alternative phrasings, identifying potential grammatical errors, and ensuring document consistency. Proofreading involves a combination of precision and creativity, enabling you to refine content until it's flawless!

How to Use ChatGPT:

- **Suggest Alternative Sentence Structures:** Improve clarity and flow by refining sentence structure.

- **Identify Inconsistencies:** Spot grammatical or stylistic inconsistencies across documents.
- **Recommend Synonyms:** Keep content fresh by suggesting synonyms for overused words.
- **Create Style Guides:** Assist in creating style guides for consistency in tone and language.

Potential Earnings:

$20-$40 per hour, depending on the type of content and your expertise.

Platforms to Use:

- **Grammarly:** Supplement your manual proofreading with this tool to catch grammar and style issues.
- **ProWritingAid:** Another excellent tool for improving clarity and consistency.
- **Upwork** or **Fiverr:** Ideal for finding freelance clients.

Quick-Start Steps:

1. **Master Grammar Rules:** Deepen your understanding of grammar and familiarize yourself with major style guides (e.g., Chicago Manual of Style, AP Style).
2. **Gain Experience:** Start proofreading various content, such as academic papers, business documents, and creative writing.
3. **Boost Credentials:** Take online courses or obtain editing certifications to enhance credibility.
4. **Build Your Presence:** Set up profiles on freelance platforms or network with publishing houses and authors.

Tips for Success:

- **Cross-check Suggestions:** Always verify ChatGPT's suggestions with authoritative style guides to ensure accuracy.
- **Cultivate Meticulous Attention to Detail:** Every word counts, so develop a sharp eye for the finer points.
- **Stay Current:** Keep up with language developments and specialized terminology in different industries.
- **Educate Clients:** Inform clients about the differences between proofreading and editing to emphasize the value of your services.

Proofreading is transforming rough drafts into polished masterpieces. As you specialize in certain types of content – academic, business, or creative writing – you'll become a go-to expert for high-quality editing. Focus on building a solid reputation for precision and reliability, which will attract long-term clients and word-of-mouth referrals. Engage with professional editing networks to stay connected and keep advancing in your side hustle.

Art & Design Side Hustles

"Creativity takes courage."

Henri Matisse

This section explores side hustles that tap into both artistic creativity and design expertise. From logo design to custom illustrations, AI tools like DALL-E and ChatGPT can enhance your creative process, helping you generate ideas, explore color schemes, and refine compositions. Whether you're crafting eye-catching visuals for t-shirts, book covers, or infographics, your unique expertise elevates these AI-assisted concepts into polished, professional works. This section will guide you on utilizing AI to boost productivity and foster creativity. Dive into the exciting world of art and design, and turn your artistic passion into a thriving side hustle!

21. Logo Design

Creating a brand's visual identity is an opportunity for creativity to thrive, and logo design offers the perfect canvas. Imagine crafting memorable, impactful logos that embody a business's values and vision. While AI tools like DALL-E can't replace your unique design intuition, they can supercharge your process – helping you generate initial concepts, explore color schemes, and ignite fresh inspiration. Your expertise will transform these ideas into polished, professional logos that stand out in any industry!

How to Use DALL-E:

- **Generate Initial Concepts:** Start by feeding DALL-E a business description and generate unique logo ideas.
- **Explore Color Schemes:** Experiment with various color combinations that align with the brand's identity.
- **Create Abstract Icons:** Let DALL-E help you visualize industry-specific logo icons or abstract shapes.
- **Visualize Typography Styles:** Try different font styles to find the perfect one for your client's brand name.

Potential Earnings:

$20 to $300+ per logo, depending on the client, complexity, and your expertise.

Platforms to Use:

- **99Designs:** Connect with clients specifically looking for logo and branding design.
- **Fiverr:** Offer logo design services to various clients across industries.
- **Upwork:** Find freelance gigs or long-term design projects.
- **Behance:** Showcase your portfolio and network with potential clients.
- **Dribbble:** Join a community of designers to display your work and find opportunities.
- **Local Networking:** Reach out to businesses in your area or use your website to attract clients.

Quick-Start Steps:

1. **Master Logo Design Principles:** Study logo design essentials, including typography and color theory.
2. **Practice with DALL-E:** Experiment with generating logo concepts and refine them into final designs.
3. **Build a Portfolio:** Create a portfolio showcasing your ability to merge AI concepts with your creative design skills.
4. **Get Your Name Out There:** Set up profiles on freelance platforms, join design communities, or contact local businesses directly.

Tips for Success:

- **Refine AI Outputs:** Use DALL-E as a springboard – your human creativity is the real magic that turns concepts into powerful logos.
- **Tailor Every Logo:** Each design should be unique and deeply connected to the brand's personality.
- **Communicate Effectively with Clients:** Clearly articulate your design choices to show clients why your work stands out.
- **Stay on Top of Trends:** Stay updated on the latest logo design trends and industry best practices.

Logo design is about telling a brand's story through a single image; it's not just about aesthetics. With AI to help you brainstorm and your creativity leading the way, you can craft logos that leave a lasting impression. As you specialize in certain styles or industries, you'll become a go-to expert, building a reputation for originality and precision. Develop complementary skills, such as brand identity or packaging design, to expand your services and keep your clients coming back for more. Dive into design communities to gain feedback, share ideas, and keep pushing the boundaries of your creativity!

22. T-shirt Design

Do you love T-shirts and have some great ideas? T-shirt design is all about transforming those ideas into eye-catching, marketable graphics for apparel. With DALL-E, you can spark fresh design concepts, explore various visual styles, and craft unique illustrations. Your expertise turns AI-generated ideas into polished, print-ready designs that resonate with audiences and look fantastic on fabric.

How to Use DALL-E:

- **Generate Initial Concepts:** Use DALL-E to create visual ideas based on popular themes or catchy slogans.
- **Create Unique Illustrations:** Let DALL-E generate one-of-a-kind illustrations or characters for your graphic tees.
- **Explore Typography Styles:** Experiment with different font styles to see what fits your text-based designs.
- **Visualize Color Schemes:** Try various color combinations to ensure your designs pop on fabric.

Potential Earnings:

$4+ per shirt, so if you sell 100 shirts, you can make an easy $400.00 from one design.

Platforms to Use:

- **Redbubble:** Sell your designs on a range of products, including T-shirts.
- **Teespring (now Spring):** Create custom merchandise with no upfront costs.
- **Etsy:** Perfect for direct sales and connecting with a niche market.
- **Printify:** Link your designs to platforms like Shopify, Walmart, and WooCommerce for broader sales opportunities.

Quick-Start Steps:

1. **Study Trends:** Familiarize yourself with current T-shirt design trends and popular printing techniques.
2. **Practice with DALL-E:** Use DALL-E to generate unique design concepts and refine them into market-ready art.
3. **Build Your Portfolio:** Create a portfolio showcasing your designs, combining AI-generated elements with your style.
4. **Launch Your Store:** Set up accounts on print-on-demand platforms or contact local businesses looking for custom T-shirt designs.

Tips for Success:

- **Refine AI Outputs:** Use DALL-E as a springboard – your human creativity is what turns concepts into standout T-shirt designs.
- **Design for Your Audience:** Know your target audience and design with them in mind for maximum appeal.

- **Understand Printing Methods:** Learn various printing techniques to ensure your designs translate well onto fabric.
- **Stay Trendy:** Look to pop culture and trending topics for inspiration that could lead to marketable designs.

Creating graphics that connect with your audience and work well on fabric is essential when designing apparel. While DALL-E is a powerful tool to spark your creativity, your expertise ensures these designs stand out in the competitive fashion world. Consider focusing on specific niches or styles and build your brand through social media or print-on-demand platforms. Uphold ethical standards by respecting copyright laws and ensuring your designs are original, even with AI-generated elements. Refining your designs based on audience feedback can help turn your T-shirt ideas into a successful business!

23. Book Cover Design

If you enjoy creating captivating visual representations of stories, book cover design could be your dream side hustle. It's all about crafting eye-catching covers that capture the essence of a book and entice readers in a competitive market. With DALL-E, you can generate stunning visual concepts, explore a variety of styles, and create one-of-a-kind imagery. Your magic lies in turning those AI-generated ideas into polished, market-ready covers that resonate with readers across different genres.

How to Use DALL-E:

- **Generate Visual Concepts:** Input book titles or synopses into DALL-E to spark creative ideas.
- **Create Unique Imagery:** Develop abstract designs or thematic illustrations that align with the book's storyline.
- **Explore Typography Styles:** Experiment with different fonts for book titles and author names.
- **Visualize Color Schemes:** Try various color palettes and compositions to fit the genre and tone.

Potential Earnings:

- $50 - $300+ per cover, depending on the client, complexity, and your expertise.

Platforms to Use:

- **Amazon Kindle Direct Publishing:** A hub for self-published authors.
- **Reedsy:** Connect with authors looking for professional cover design.
- **99Designs:** Participate in design contests or find new clients.
- **Fiverr:** Offer your services to clients across the globe.

Quick-Start Steps:

1. **Study Genre-Specific Covers:** Research successful book covers in different literary genres to understand trends and reader expectations.

2. **Master Typography and Color Theory:** Learn how typography and color impact book marketing.

3. **Practice with DALL-E:** Generate cover concepts to sharpen your skills.

4. **Create a Portfolio:** Design sample book covers for various genres to showcase your versatility.

Tips for Success:

- **Refine AI Outputs:** Use DALL-E for inspiration, but fine-tune designs to meet industry standards.

- **Understand Genre Conventions:** Know the nuances of each genre's cover design to appeal to target readers.

- **Learn Technical Requirements:** Ensure your designs meet the technical specs for both print and digital formats.

- **Develop Typography Skills:** Strong typography is vital to professional, appealing book covers.

- Book cover design is about creating a visual hook that draws readers in. While DALL-E can kickstart your creative process, your design skills will bring the covers to life. As you grow in this field, consider specializing in specific genres to enhance your expertise further. Build strong relationships with authors and publishers to foster long-term collaborations and stay updated on design trends to continue offering fresh, market-ready book covers.

24. Poster Design and Printables

Are you driven by the challenge of creating bold, eye-catching designs that make an impact and communicate a clear message? Poster design is a perfect way to channel creativity for events, advertisements, home decor, or printables like motivational quotes and organizational tools. With DALL-E as your creative assistant, you can quickly generate initial concepts, experiment with various artistic styles, and transform unique ideas into stunning visuals. Your expertise transforms these AI-generated concepts into polished, impactful posters and printables that captivate viewers and communicate the intended message.

How to Use DALL-E:

- **Generate Visual Concepts:** Feed DALL-E event themes, product descriptions, or inspirational quotes to create a base for your designs.

- **Create Unique Illustrations:** Generate illustrations or abstract designs tailored to the poster or printable's purpose.

- **Explore Layout Options:** Visualize different compositions and find the most effective arrangement of elements.

- **Experiment with Color Schemes:** Play with various colors and styles to evoke the right mood and tone for your designs.

Potential Earnings:

- $10+ per poster or printable, depending on whether you sell POD (Print On Demand), offer digital downloads, or work directly with clients. Bundling multiple printables can increase sales.

Platforms to Use:

- **Etsy:** Ideal for selling physical posters and digital printables like wall art, motivational quotes, and organizational tools.
- **Zazzle** or **Printful:** Perfect for print-on-demand poster sales.
- **Creative Market:** Sell high-quality printables to a more design-focused audience.
- **Upwork** or **Fiverr:** Find clients who need custom poster designs.

Quick-Start Steps:

1. **Study Poster Design Trends:** Familiarize yourself with practical designs for events, movies, advertisements, home decor, and more.
2. **Learn Design Principles:** Master composition, typography, and color theory to make your designs stand out.
3. **Practice with DALL-E:** Use DALL-E to generate poster and printable concepts that spark inspiration.
4. **Build Your Portfolio:** Create diverse sample posters and printables to showcase your skills across various industries.

Tips for Success:

- **Refine AI Outputs:** Use DALL-E's suggestions as a starting point, then elevate them with your professional touch.
- **Balance Visuals and Information:** Ensure your designs are visually appealing and easy to understand, whether for posters or printables.
- **Understand Printing Processes:** Know how different printing methods affect your designs and plan accordingly, especially for print-on-demand.
- **Stay Updated on Trends:** Monitor design trends, pop culture, and organizational tools to create posters and printables that resonate with current audiences.

Remember, DALL-E is your creative partner, but your unique design skills and artistic vision will set your posters and printables apart. Success lies in blending AI inspiration with your flair to create stunning, professional designs that captivate and resonate. Whether you specialize in event posters, decorative wall art, or digital printables, mastering your craft will boost your reputation and earning potential. As you build a portfolio of eye-catching designs and expand your product offerings, you'll attract clients, grow your audience, and watch your design side hustle thrive!

25. Custom Illustrations

Imagine turning someone's ideas into vivid, eye-catching artwork tailored to their needs! Custom illustration creates unique visuals for books, magazines, websites, and products. DALL-E can help kickstart the creative process by generating initial concepts, exploring artistic styles, and laying the groundwork for your illustrations. But your artistic skill transforms these ideas into polished, professional pieces that leave a lasting impression.

How to Use DALL-E:

- **Generate Initial Concepts:** Kick off with client briefs or story descriptions to inspire creative directions.
- **Explore Artistic Styles:** Experiment with various visual aesthetics and color palettes to match the project.
- **Create Base Compositions:** Use DALL-E to lay down background elements or structure the overall design.
- **Visualize Characters or Products:** Create detailed character or product visuals that fully capture and realize the client's vision.

Potential Earnings:

- $50 - $1000+ per illustration, depending on complexity, usage rights, and your expertise.

Platforms to Use:

- **DeviantArt:** Perfect for showcasing your unique illustrations and connecting with clients.
- **ArtStation:** A professional portfolio platform with job listings to match.
- **Upwork** & **Fiverr:** Great for finding freelance custom illustration gigs.

Quick-Start Steps:

1. **Find Your Style:** Cultivate your distinctive illustration style (or diversify across genres).
2. **Learn the Tools:** Combine DALL-E with digital illustration software for a more streamlined process.
3. **Build a Portfolio:** Create and showcase a collection of AI-assisted illustrations in various niches.
4. **Create Profiles:** Set up accounts on art platforms and freelance sites to market your services.

Tips for Success:

- **Enhance AI Ideas:** Use AI-generated concepts as a foundation, but let your creativity define the final product.
- **Master Refinement:** Focus on refining and perfecting your illustrations to exceed client expectations.

- **Know Your Medium:** Familiarize yourself with different illustration applications, such as editorial, product design, or children's books.
- **Keep Learning:** Stay updated on the latest illustration trends and techniques to stand out in a competitive market.

Creating custom illustrations goes beyond just drawing; it's understanding and translating a client's vision into stunning visuals. While DALL-E helps jumpstart the process, your skill and expertise in refining these ideas into one-of-a-kind artwork set you apart. Whether you focus on specific genres or expand into diverse projects, combining AI's potential with your artistic talent is the key to success. Building solid relationships with clients and continually evolving your skills will ensure a thriving career in custom illustration.

26. Infographic Design

Infographic design transforms complex data into visually appealing, easy-to-digest graphics that tell a compelling story. Imagine transforming dense information into something engaging and visually stunning! With DALL-E and ChatGPT, you can shape your ideas into reality by generating initial design concepts, creating impactful data visualizations, and drafting clear, concise content. Your expertise refines these AI-generated elements, ensuring that your infographics captivate and inform audiences at a glance.

How to Use AI Tools:

- **Visual Metaphors:** Use DALL-E to create eye-catching icons or metaphors to represent your topic.
- **Layouts and Colors:** Generate base layouts and explore color schemes with DALL-E for stunning designs.
- **Text Summaries:** Have ChatGPT condense complex information into clear, concise explanations.
- **Data Visualization Ideas:** Let ChatGPT inspire creative formats for showcasing your data.

Potential Earnings:

- $35 - $100+ per hour, depending on the client and your expertise.

Platforms to Use:

- **Canva:** Great for creating simple infographics with ease.
- **Venngage:** Excellent for professional-quality templates and data visualization tools.
- **Upwork** & **Fiverr:** Perfect for finding freelance clients who need your design expertise.

Quick-Start Steps:

1. **Study Infographic Design:** Understand the principles of effective infographic creation and data visualization.

2. **Master the Tools:** Get comfortable with design software and infographic-specific tools like Canva and Venngage.
3. **Create and Practice:** Use AI tools to assist with your first infographics and build a portfolio showcasing your style.
4. **Get Noticed:** Set up profiles on freelance platforms and pitch to potential clients.

Tips for Success:

- **Refine AI Outputs:** Use AI-generated visuals as a starting point, then polish them for professional clarity.
- **Data Accuracy:** Always fact-check and ensure the accuracy of the data you present, and cite your sources.
- **Balance, Beauty, and Clarity:** A great infographic is not just pretty – it communicates complex ideas clearly and effectively.
- **Stay Ahead of Trends:** Follow the latest data visualization trends to keep your designs fresh and relevant.

Infographic design is about transforming data into stories that captivate and engage. While DALL-E and ChatGPT can provide a starting point, your design expertise and data interpretation skills will bring those stories to fruition. Specializing in specific industries or types of infographics can set you apart, and maintaining accuracy and originality will solidify your reputation in the field. Build a strong portfolio and network with potential clients, and you'll be on your way to infographic design success!

27. Website Design

Website design offers the chance to blend creativity with functionality, crafting visually appealing, user-friendly websites that help businesses thrive. With AI tools like DALL-E and ChatGPT, you can spark initial design concepts, generate stunning visual elements, and draft compelling copy. But your expertise as a web designer transforms these ideas into polished, cohesive websites that meet your client's goals while delivering an exceptional user experience.

How to Use AI Tools:

- **Generate Layout Concepts:** Use DALL-E to visualize website layouts, color schemes, and design ideas.
- **Create Unique Imagery:** Design custom icons, banners, or visual elements with DALL-E for added flair.
- **Draft Website Copy:** Let ChatGPT assist in crafting attention-grabbing headlines, compelling CTAs, and informative content.
- **Plan Site Structure:** Use ChatGPT to brainstorm site architecture, user flow, and navigation strategies.

Potential Earnings:

- $30-$80 per hour, depending on complexity, features, and expertise. Ongoing maintenance can provide additional income.

Platforms to Use:

- **Wix:** For building visually stunning and functional websites.
- **Squarespace:** To create and manage stylish, professional websites.
- **Upwork** or **Freelancer:** To connect with clients seeking web design services.

Quick-Start Steps:

1. **Master Web Design Principles:** Learn about UX/UI design, website responsiveness, and core design concepts.
2. **Familiarize Yourself with Tools:** Get hands-on with website builders and basic HTML/CSS.
3. **Create Sample Websites:** Use AI to assist in building mock websites to showcase your design range.
4. **Build a Portfolio:** Highlight your versatility by displaying different types of websites.

Tips for Success:

- **Refine AI Outputs:** Use AI-generated ideas as inspiration, but tailor each design to your client's specific needs.
- **Prioritize User Experience:** Ensure your designs are intuitive and user-friendly.
- **Learn Responsive Design:** Focus on creating websites that work seamlessly across devices.
- **Stay Current:** Keep up with the latest web design trends, tools, and techniques.

While AI can enhance your workflow by generating design concepts and copy, your talent as a web designer is the key to turning those ideas into websites that stand out. Specializing in niches like e-commerce, portfolios, or blogs can set you apart, while expanding your knowledge in areas like SEO and accessibility can elevate your services. Create memorable user experiences that help businesses succeed online, and you'll build lasting relationships and a strong reputation in the web design world.

28. Social Media Graphics

Have you ever scrolled through Instagram or Facebook and stopped because a stunning image caught your eye? That's the power of social media graphics – turning casual scrollers into engaged followers. Now, imagine being the one behind those attention-grabbing visuals! With AI tools like DALL-E and ChatGPT, you can transform bold ideas into reality by generating fresh design concepts, creating unique visuals, and crafting engaging captions. Your expertise takes those AI-generated ideas and transforms them into polished, platform-specific graphics that not only look great but also drive engagement and brand awareness.

How to Use AI Tools:

- **Generate Visual Concepts:** Use DALL-E to create design ideas based on content themes or brand guidelines.
- **Create Unique Imagery:** Design illustrations, backgrounds, or icons with DALL-E to add flair to your graphics.
- **Draft Captions:** Let ChatGPT assist in writing attention-grabbing captions that complement your visuals.
- **Brainstorm Themed Content:** Use ChatGPT to generate ideas for post series or seasonal content themes.

Potential Earnings:

- $5 - $100+ per graphic, or $300 - $1500+ for social media graphic packages, depending on the volume and complexity.

Platforms to Use:

- **Canva:** A user-friendly design tool for social media content.
- **Adobe Express:** Ideal for crafting polished social media graphics.
- **Instagram**, **Facebook**, and **LinkedIn**: Showcase your work and attract clients through these platforms.

Quick-Start Steps:

1. **Master Platform Specs:** Learn about different social media platforms' image sizes and design specifications.
2. **Study Visual Trends:** Analyze successful social media campaigns to understand what works.
3. **Build a Portfolio:** Create sample graphics for various industries and social platforms.
4. **Get Clients:** Set up profiles on freelance platforms or connect with small businesses needing social media design.

Tips for Success:

- **Refine AI Outputs:** Use AI-generated visuals as inspiration, then tweak them to match brand guidelines and platform needs.
- **Understand Platform Language:** Tailor your designs to each social media platform's unique aesthetic and language.
- **Master Social Media Strategy:** Learn how design fits broader social media marketing efforts to create impactful content.
- **Stay Trendy:** Keep up with social media trends and algorithm changes to ensure your designs stay relevant.

AI can jumpstart your creative process, but your real superpower is transforming those concepts into visually striking graphics that tell a brand's story. As you build your skills, consider specializing in a particular niche – whether it's creating Instagram stories for beauty brands or Facebook ads for local businesses. Understanding social media strategy is critical to creating content that grabs attention and drives action. By consistently creating visually engaging designs and staying current with social media trends, you'll be a go-to designer for brands looking to stand out.

29. Custom Wallpaper Design

Imagine seeing your creative designs transform into stunning wall art that brings life to homes, offices, or commercial spaces. Custom wallpaper design is all about creating one-of-a-kind, large-scale patterns that completely transform any room. With DALL-E, you can spark your creativity, generate unique visual concepts, and explore various color schemes. But the magic happens when you refine those AI-generated ideas into polished, repeatable patterns that fit perfectly into a client's style and vision.

How to Use DALL-E:

- **Generate Pattern Ideas:** Start with style or theme descriptions to create the perfect visual inspiration.
- **Create Unique Visual Elements:** Design original illustrations or shapes to incorporate into your patterns.
- **Explore Color Combinations:** Try color schemes to match the mood and space.
- **Visualize Patterns in Rooms:** See how your designs could look in various settings, from living rooms to commercial spaces.

Potential Earnings:

$15-$35+ per hour or charge per design. Earnings depend on complexity, client type, and whether you sell directly or through print-on-demand. You could even earn royalties if your designs are mass-produced.

Platforms to Use:

- **Society6:** Sell your wallpaper designs directly to consumers.
- **Spoonflower:** Offer custom fabric and wallpaper for printing.
- **Etsy:** Sell digital wallpaper files for DIYers and interior enthusiasts.

Quick-Start Steps:

1. **Study Trends:** Explore current wallpaper trends and design principles.
2. **Learn Repeat Patterns:** Understand how to create seamless, large-scale designs.
3. **Build a Portfolio:** Use AI to enhance your creative process to develop diverse wallpaper patterns.
4. **Start Selling:** Set up on print-on-demand platforms or pitch directly to interior designers.

Tips for Success:

- **Refine for Perfection:** Use AI for inspiration but perfect your designs for seamless repetition and ideal scale.
- **Understand Interior Styles:** Know how different spaces and styles can be complemented with wallpaper.
- **Master Printing Techniques:** Learn about wallpaper printing methods to optimize your designs.
- **Stay on Trend:** Follow the latest interior design and color trends to keep your work fresh.

By tapping into the world of custom wallpaper design, you can bring your artistic visions into real-world spaces. Whether specializing in botanical, geometric, or minimalist designs, AI will support your creative flow. Still, your artistic refinement and eye for detail will make your work stand out. Forge relationships with interior designers or decorators, and stay connected with the design community to grow your exposure and success!

30. Business Card Design

Think about a well-designed business card's impact – it's often the first impression someone gets of a business. That's why creating visually stunning, memorable cards is such a rewarding experience. If you love combining creativity with practicality, this could be your niche! With AI tools like DALL-E and ChatGPT, you can take your designs to the next level by generating visual concepts, color schemes, and clever copy. The result? Business cards that stand out represent a brand's identity and leave a lasting impression.

How to Use AI Tools:

- **Generate Visual Concepts:** Use DALL-E to create ideas based on the business's industry or brand identity.
- **Create Unique Icons or Backgrounds:** Develop abstract designs or icons with DALL-E for eye-catching backgrounds.
- **Craft Taglines and Descriptions:** ChatGPT can help brainstorm memorable taglines or concise business descriptions.
- **Design Layouts and Typography:** Generate ideas for the card's layout and typography using ChatGPT.

Potential Earnings:

$50 - $2500+ per design, depending on complexity, client, and your expertise.

Platforms to Use:

- **Vistaprint:** This is for printing and potential client referrals.
- **Moo:** For high-quality printing services and inspiration.
- **Fiverr** or **99Designs:** Perfect for finding clients who need custom business card designs.

Quick-Start Steps:

1. **Study Successful Designs:** Analyze different industries' business card trends to understand what works.
2. **Learn About Printing:** Understand how printing techniques and materials affect design choices.
3. **Create a Portfolio:** Design sample business cards for various professions and industries.
4. **Network with Local Businesses:** Set up freelance profiles or reach out to businesses in your community.

Tips for Success:

- **Refine for Brand Consistency:** AI provides an excellent foundation, but your expertise ensures the design aligns with the brand.
- **Focus on Practicality:** Ensure all necessary information is clear and accessible.
- **Know Your Paper and Finishes:** Educate yourself on paper stocks and unique finishes to elevate your designs.
- **Stay Current:** Keep an eye on design trends and best practices for business cards.

While AI can help with initial design concepts, your skill lies in understanding branding and translating that into a small but powerful medium – business cards. As you grow, consider specializing in premium materials or specific industries. Always be transparent with clients about AI usage, and build lasting relationships by delivering professional, standout designs. With the right approach, you can transform a simple business card into a powerful networking tool.

31. Digital Art Sales

Imagine turning your creativity into a thriving digital art business! If you're passionate about creating visual art and love the idea of selling your work online, this could be the perfect side hustle for you. With tools like DALL-E, you can generate initial concepts, explore different styles, and build on those ideas to create stunning, unique pieces. Your role? To transform these AI-generated elements into digital masterpieces that reflect your artistic vision, ready to captivate audiences and sell worldwide.

How to Use AI Tools:

- **Generate Visual Concepts:** Use DALL-E to get inspiration or base ideas for your artwork.
- **Create Base Elements:** Build backgrounds, patterns, or abstract shapes to customize further.
- **Explore Artistic Styles:** Experiment with color palettes and different artistic approaches.
- **Design Variations:** Use DALL-E to create multiple concept versions and refine the best.

Potential Earnings:

$50 - $1000+ per piece, or $1000 - $10,000+ per month, depending on style, marketing efforts, and demand.

Platforms to Use:

- **DeviantArt:** Showcase and sell your digital art.
- **ArtStation:** Build a professional portfolio and access potential buyers.
- **Etsy:** Perfect for selling digital downloads of your artwork.

Quick-Start Steps:

1. **Develop Your Style:** Blend your unique touch with AI elements to create standout digital art.
2. **Build a Portfolio:** Showcase your best work, including AI-assisted designs.
3. **Set Up Sales Platforms:** Get started on DeviantArt, ArtStation, or Etsy to reach buyers.
4. **Master Licensing & Pricing:** Learn the ins and outs of selling and licensing digital art.

Tips for Success:

- **Blend AI with Personal Creativity:** Use AI as inspiration, but make sure your artistic voice shines through.
- **Engage with the Community:** Connect with other digital artists and potential buyers to grow your fan base.
- **Understand File Formats:** Ensure your art is available in the correct formats and resolutions for various buyers.
- **Leverage Social Media:** Use Instagram, Twitter, and Pinterest to share your art and attract buyers.

While AI can spark initial ideas, your talent and creativity will transform them into something remarkable. Use AI tools to enhance, not replace, your artistic process, and always infuse your unique style into each piece. Consider focusing on specific digital art niches like character design, surreal landscapes, or NFTs. Master digital marketing strategies, understand copyright laws, and actively engage with your audience. By building a solid presence on digital platforms and consistently producing eye-catching art, you'll develop a loyal following and grow your sales over time. Stay connected with the digital art world, collaborate with fellow creators, and continue refining your craft to stay ahead in this ever-evolving field.

32. Photography

Photography could be your ideal side hustle if you've ever felt the thrill of capturing a perfect moment through your lens! Whether shooting weddings, creating stock images, or snapping breathtaking portraits, photography lets you channel your creativity while earning an income. With AI tools like DALL-E to inspire fresh compositions and ChatGPT to assist with captions and metadata, you can take your photography game to the next level – streamlining your process and opening up more opportunities to showcase your talent.

How to Use AI Tools:

- **Generate Visual Concepts:** Use DALL-E to explore unique composition ideas or themes for your shoots.
- **Write Captions and Descriptions:** Let ChatGPT help you craft compelling photo captions and descriptions.
- **Enhance Searchability:** Use ChatGPT to generate keywords and metadata, making your stock images more straightforward to find.
- **Create Editing Presets:** Develop AI-assisted presets for consistent editing across multiple photos.

Potential Earnings:

This varies based on the niche. Earn $5,000+ for a wedding, $25 - $45+ per hour for product photography, or up to $120+ per image for stock photography.

Platforms to Use:

- **Adobe Lightroom:** Ideal for editing and managing your photo library.
- **Shutterstock** or **Getty Images:** For selling stock photos and earning royalties.
- **Instagram** or **Flickr:** Showcase your portfolio and connect with potential clients.

Quick-Start Steps:

1. **Develop Your Skills:** Hone your photography techniques and find your niche – whether it's weddings, events, or products.
2. **Invest in Equipment:** Quality cameras and editing software are essential to deliver professional results.
3. **Build a Portfolio:** Showcase your best work in a diverse online portfolio.
4. **Join Job Boards:** Sign up on photography platforms or stock photo sites to start selling and booking gigs.

Tips for Success:

- **Use AI for Inspiration:** Let AI spark ideas, but always stay true to your unique creative vision.
- **Create a Consistent Style:** Develop a signature editing style to establish a recognizable brand.
- **Understand Licensing:** Learn the ins and outs of copyright and image licensing to protect your work.
- **Network Locally:** Build connections with event planners, businesses, and clients in your area for more opportunities

AI tools can spark new ideas, simplify workflow, and help with technical aspects like tagging and writing captions, but your eye for detail and passion for storytelling through images genuinely make your photography stand out. As you grow, consider specializing in wedding photography, real estate, or stock images. Stay transparent about AI use, protect your work through proper licensing, and engage with the creative community. By building your portfolio, networking, and consistently producing stunning visuals, you'll carve out a successful niche in photography.

33. Videography

If you love capturing moments in motion and telling stories through video, videography could be your perfect creative outlet! Whether filming weddings, creating marketing videos, or producing content for YouTube, videography allows you to merge technical skills with artistry. By integrating AI tools like ChatGPT, you can elevate your services – generating script ideas, streamlining your production process, and refining your editing techniques. It's all about creating visually stunning, impactful videos that leave a lasting impression on your audience.

How to Use AI Tools:

- **Generate Video Concepts:** Let ChatGPT help you brainstorm creative ideas and storyboards for your videos.
- **Create Script Outlines:** Draft scripts and narration with AI-generated dialogue suggestions.
- **Develop Shot Lists:** Use AI to create comprehensive shot lists, ensuring you capture all critical moments.
- **Enhance Searchability:** Write video descriptions and generate tags with ChatGPT for better online visibility.

Potential Earnings:

- Earnings vary based on experience and project scope, but you can expect around $2,500 for a three-minute video. Freelancers on platforms like Upwork typically earn between $10 - $53 per hour.

Platforms to Use:

- **Adobe Premiere Pro** or **Final Cut Pro:** For professional video editing and production.
- **YouTube** or **Vimeo:** Showcase your portfolio and attract new clients.
- **Upwork** or **Fiverr:** Find videography gigs and build your client base.

Quick-Start Steps:

1. **Master Your Craft:** Develop shooting and editing skills to produce high-quality videos.
2. **Invest in Equipment:** Quality cameras, lighting, and editing software are vital to delivering professional results.
3. **Build a Demo Reel:** Highlight your best work in a short reel that showcases your versatility.

4. **Network Locally:** Connect with businesses and event planners to expand your project opportunities.

Tips for Success:

- **Leverage AI, but Stay Creative:** Use AI tools to streamline processes, but always bring your unique vision.
- **Stay Updated:** Keep up with the latest videography trends and editing techniques.
- **Optimize for Platforms:** Learn the best video formats and optimizations for platforms like YouTube, Instagram, and more.
- **Focus on Storytelling:** Strong storytelling makes videos genuinely memorable and impactful.

While AI can enhance efficiency and creativity in videography, your true value is capturing compelling visuals, directing powerful narratives, and transforming each client's vision into reality. Specializing in certain types of videography – events, corporate projects, or content creation – can give you a competitive edge. Stay connected with evolving tech trends, develop strong client relationships, and continuously hone your skills to make a lasting mark in this dynamic industry!

Marketing & Advertising Side Hustles

"Doing business without advertising is like winking at someone in the dark. You know what you're doing, but nobody else does."

Stuart H. Britt

Marketing and advertising offer dynamic side hustle opportunities for those who excel at creating impactful campaigns and engaging audiences. Whether managing social media, crafting email campaigns, or running targeted ads, combining creativity with strategy is critical. By leveraging AI tools like ChatGPT, you can streamline your workflow, brainstorm fresh ideas, and optimize content. This section will guide you through various ways to turn your marketing and advertising skills into profitable ventures, helping businesses connect with their audiences and achieve their goals.

34. Social Media Management

If you have a strong interest in social media and enjoy creating engaging content, social media management could be your ideal side hustle! Managing a brand's online presence goes beyond just posting; it's about creating connections, building communities, and delivering value to audiences. By leveraging AI tools like ChatGPT and DALL-E, you can boost your creativity, streamline content creation, and maximize efficiency, all while ensuring each client's social media presence stands out in a crowded digital space.

How to Use AI Tools:

- **Generate Post Ideas:** Use ChatGPT to brainstorm creative post ideas and draft captions tailored to each platform.
- **Create Visuals:** Leverage DALL-E to design eye-catching visuals and graphics that resonate with the audience.
- **Engage with Audiences:** Have ChatGPT assist in crafting thoughtful responses to comments, messages, and inquiries.
- **Plan and Schedule:** Use AI to develop content calendars and posting schedules, ensuring consistency across platforms.

Potential Earnings:

- $35+ per hour, depending on your level of expertise and the range of services you offer.

Platforms to Use:

- **Hootsuite:** This is for managing multiple platforms and scheduling posts.
- **Buffer:** A tool for content planning, publishing, and analytics.
- **Sprout Social:** For more profound insights into social media performance and audience engagement.

Quick-Start Steps:

1. **Master Social Media Platforms:** Learn the ins and outs of major platforms like **Instagram**, **Facebook**, **LinkedIn**, **TikTok**, and **X (formerly known as Twitter)**.
2. **Use Social Media Tools:** Familiarize yourself with social media management tools like **Hootsuite** and **Buffer** to streamline your processes.
3. **Build Sample Campaigns:** Create mock social media campaigns for different types of businesses to showcase your skills.
4. **Reach Out to Clients:** Set up profiles on freelance platforms or directly approach local businesses to offer your services.

Tips for Success:

- **Customize AI Outputs:** Use AI-generated content as a starting point, but constantly tailor it to match the client's brand voice and audience.
- **Stay on Trend:** Keep up with the latest social media trends, platform updates, and algorithm changes.
- **Develop Analytical Skills:** Understanding social media analytics is key to refining strategies and improving engagement.
- **Network for Growth:** Build a portfolio of diverse social media campaigns and cultivate relationships with clients in various industries.

As a social media manager, your value lies in crafting strategies that align with business goals while creating authentic engagement with audiences. Use AI to save time and spark creativity, but your human touch in understanding audience behaviors, trends, and storytelling is irreplaceable. Specialize in industries that interest you, develop influencer marketing skills, and stay adaptable in this fast-paced field. Over time, building strong client relationships and staying ahead of digital trends will lead to long-term success and opportunities for growth!

35. Email Marketing

Imagine being the person who delivers the perfect message at the ideal time directly into someone's inbox! Email marketing gives you the power to engage, inspire, and drive action – all through carefully crafted emails. With AI tools like ChatGPT, you can brainstorm fresh ideas, write compelling copy, and personalize your messages, helping you create email campaigns that connect with your audience. Your role is to turn these AI-generated ideas into tailored, high-impact emails that leave a lasting impression.

How to Use AI Tools:

- **Generate Subject Lines & Preview Text:** Use ChatGPT to brainstorm captivating subject lines and previews that increase open rates.
- **Draft Body Content:** Collaborate with AI to write engaging content while maintaining your unique touch and voice.
- **Personalize for Audience Segments:** Tailor content to different subscriber groups for more effective engagement.
- **Design Email Series:** Use AI to plan multi-step drip campaigns that nurture leads over time.

Potential Earnings:

$25 to $100 per hour, depending on your work scope and expertise.

Platforms to Use:

- **Mailchimp:** Ideal for campaign creation and management.
- **Active Campaign:** Perfect for advanced automation and marketing strategies.
- **MailerLite:** A more straightforward tool with great automation features.
- **ConvertKit:** Popular among content creators and bloggers.

Quick-Start Steps:

1. **Master Email Marketing Regulations:** Familiarize yourself with email regulations like CAN-SPAM and GDPR.
2. **Learn Popular Platforms:** Practice using email marketing platforms and automation features.
3. **Build a Portfolio:** Create sample campaigns for various industries to showcase your skills.
4. **Find Clients:** Set up freelance profiles or approach local businesses needing email marketing support.

Tips for Success:

- **Refine AI Content:** Always edit AI-generated copy to ensure it matches the client's brand and voice.
- **Focus on Strong CTAs:** Craft compelling calls-to-action that drive conversions and results.

- **Understand Deliverability:** Learn how to ensure your emails land in inboxes, not spam folders.
- **Optimize Through Data:** Use A/B testing and data analytics to refine and improve campaign performance.

Email marketing is more than just hitting "send." It's building lasting relationships and delivering meaningful content that gets results. Combining your creative vision with AI's efficiency enables you to craft email campaigns that engage, inspire, and drive action. Keep refining your strategies and leveraging AI to stay ahead of the game!

36. Ad Copy Creation

Crafting ad copy can be an exciting way to channel your creativity and persuasive skills. Imagine being responsible for creating that perfect headline or phrase that grabs attention and drives action! With AI tools like ChatGPT, you can brainstorm ideas, test multiple variations, and refine your message to connect with your audience and meet campaign goals. Your expertise turns those AI-generated ideas into compelling, high-converting ad copy that resonates with different audiences across multiple platforms.

How to Use AI Tools:

- **Generate Headline Options:** Use ChatGPT to brainstorm eye-catching headlines that stop people in their tracks.
- **Draft Ad Descriptions:** Collaborate with AI to create engaging, concise ad descriptions highlighting product or service benefits.
- **Create Copy Variations:** Write multiple ad variations for A/B testing to optimize performance.
- **Develop Ad Extensions:** Use AI to develop additional features for search ads, such as callout text or site links.

Potential Earnings:

- $19 - $50+ per hour, depending on the scope and your expertise.

Platforms to Use:

- **Google Ads:** Perfect for search and display advertising.
- **Facebook Ads Manager:** Great for running social media ad campaigns.
- **LinkedIn Campaign Manager:** Ideal for B2B advertising.

Quick-Start Steps:

1. **Study Ad Copy:** Analyze effective ad campaigns across platforms and industries.
2. **Learn Ad Formats:** Familiarize yourself with each platform's ad formats and character limits.

3. **Create a Portfolio:** Develop sample ad copy for different campaigns to showcase your skills.

4. **Find Clients:** Set up profiles on freelance platforms or reach out to digital marketing agencies.

Tips for Success:

- **Refine AI Output:** Use AI as a starting point, but customize the copy to fit the brand voice and platform specifics.
- **Understand Selling Propositions:** Focus on what makes a product or service unique and highlight its key benefits.
- **Target the Right Audience:** Learn about audience segmentation and how it influences the tone and message of ad copy.
- **Master Ad Formats:** Develop your ability to write copy for various formats, including text, image, and video ads.

Compelling ad copy can make or break a marketing campaign, and while AI can speed up the creative process, your skills in understanding human behavior and brand messaging are essential. Specializing in platforms like Google or Facebook Ads and honing your skills in copy performance analysis will set you apart. Ethical, transparent advertising builds trust and loyalty, so make sure every word reflects honesty and value to your audience. With a strong portfolio and a grasp of trends, you'll be ready to thrive in the fast-paced world of ad copy creation.

37. Brand Strategy Consulting

Helping businesses shape their identity and stand out in a crowded marketplace is a rewarding challenge. Imagine guiding a company to discover its unique voice and then seeing that brand come to life, connecting with audiences and driving growth! As a brand strategy consultant, your role shapes companies' perceptions. With AI tools like ChatGPT, you can brainstorm ideas, analyze trends, and generate insights. Still, your expertise and strategic thinking refine these ideas into powerful brand strategies that make a lasting impact.

How to Use AI Tools:

- **Brainstorm Positioning Statements:** Use ChatGPT to explore brand positioning options that align with the company's mission and audience.
- **Develop Brand Personality:** Generate ideas for brand traits, tone, and voice that resonate with the target demographic.
- **Analyze Competitors:** Leverage AI to evaluate competitor messaging and identify gaps or opportunities in the market.
- **Create Key Messaging:** Draft compelling brand stories, taglines, and key messaging points that align with the brand's vision.

Potential Earnings:

$50 - $100 per hour, depending on the scope and your expertise.

Platforms to Use:

- **LinkedIn:** Network and connect with potential clients.
- **Upwork:** Find freelance consulting opportunities.
- **Your Own Website:** Showcase your brand strategy expertise and attract clients directly.

Quick-Start Steps:

1. **Study Brand Strategies:** Analyze successful brands across different industries to understand what makes them stand out.
2. **Learn Brand Elements:** Understand the core elements of brand strategy, like positioning, personality, and promise.
3. **Create Sample Documents:** Draft brand strategies for imaginary businesses to showcase your ability.
4. **Build a Network:** Attend industry events and engage with online communities to build valuable connections.

Tips for Success:

- **Use AI for Ideation:** Let AI-generated content inspire you, but always rely on your strategic insights for final recommendations.
- **Strengthen Research Skills:** Develop the ability to analyze market trends and consumer behavior.
- **Facilitate Workshops:** Learn how to lead brand workshops and conduct interviews with key stakeholders to gather insights.
- **Stay Current:** Stay current with the latest consumer psychology and marketing trends to offer fresh, relevant strategies.

Brand strategy consulting is understanding the heart of a company and helping it communicate that essence effectively. AI can inspire, but your deep understanding of market dynamics, consumer behavior, and strategic thinking is what drives actual results. Specializing in specific industries or types of brand strategy can elevate your expertise, and strong research and customer experience design skills will add even more value. Build a portfolio of successful strategies and maintain strong client relationships to build a reputation as a trusted advisor. Keep learning and adapting as brands evolve, and you'll position yourself as an indispensable partner in any company's growth journey.

38. Influencer Marketing

Influencer marketing involves creating authentic connections between brands and influencers to develop campaigns that resonate deeply with audiences. Imagine being the mastermind behind a campaign that seamlessly integrates a brand's message with the unique voice of an influencer – it's exciting to watch the magic unfold! With AI tools like ChatGPT, you can streamline the research process, generate campaign ideas, and draft outreach messages. Still, your expertise and creativity craft successful influencer partnerships that drive results.

How to Use AI Tools:

- **Generate Outreach Templates:** Use ChatGPT to create personalized outreach messages for influencers.
- **Analyze Influencer Profiles:** Leverage AI to evaluate influencers' engagement rates and audience demographics.
- **Brainstorm Campaign Ideas:** Develop creative concepts, hashtags, and themes that align with brand goals.
- **Draft Campaign Briefs:** Create guidelines and objectives for influencers to ensure campaign consistency.

Potential Earnings:

- $15 - $50 per hour (higher rates possible for large campaigns and more expertise).

Platforms to Use:

- **Instagram, TikTok, YouTube:** Key platforms for influencer campaigns.
- **Upfluence:** This is for discovering influencers and managing campaigns.
- **HypeAuditor:** For analyzing influencer metrics.
- **Upwork:** To find freelancing opportunities.

Quick-Start Steps:

1. **Study Campaigns:** Analyze successful industry influencer campaigns to understand what works.
2. **Learn FTC Guidelines:** Understand the legal requirements for influencer marketing.
3. **Create Sample Campaigns:** Develop example strategies for imaginary brands to showcase your skills.
4. **Network with Agencies:** Build relationships with marketing agencies or approach brands directly.

Tips for Success:

- **Customize Outreach:** Start with AI-generated outreach messages, but personalize them for each influencer and brand.
- **Build Relationships:** Focus on relationship-building with influencers and brands for long-term success.
- **Measure ROI:** Develop skills to track and report campaign performance metrics effectively.

- **Stay Trendy:** Keep up with social media trends and new platforms to stay ahead of the curve.

Influencer marketing thrives on authentic partnerships and creative strategies that align a brand's message with an influencer's voice. While AI can help streamline research and initial content ideas, your expertise in managing relationships, creating unique campaign ideas, and measuring success make these side hustles soar. Specialize in specific industries or platforms to hone your knowledge and stand out. Always maintain transparency and ethics, especially regarding disclosures and FTC compliance. With strong client relationships, an understanding of market trends, and a strategic approach, you can turn influencer marketing into a highly rewarding side hustle.

39. Video Marketing

Are you excited about transforming ideas into dynamic, captivating videos? Video marketing lets you do just that – crafting compelling stories that captivate audiences and promote brands, products, or services. With AI tools like ChatGPT to help you brainstorm and streamline the video production process, you can focus on creating visually stunning and engaging content that drives results. Whether it's a short TikTok or an in-depth YouTube ad, you're at the forefront of turning ideas into captivating visual stories.

How to Use AI Tools:

- **Generate Video Scripts:** Use ChatGPT to generate video script ideas and outlines that align with marketing goals.
- **Storyboard Creation:** Build storyboards based on AI-generated concepts to organize the flow of your video.
- **Optimize for Platforms:** Draft video descriptions and tags for YouTube or TikTok to boost visibility.
- **Campaign Ideas:** Use AI to brainstorm ideas for entire video series or campaigns that align with your client's brand.

Potential Earnings:

- $15 - $45+ per hour, depending on complexity and your expertise.

Platforms to Use:

- **YouTube:** Great for hosting videos and leveraging ads for monetization.
- **Vimeo:** For more professional, high-quality video hosting.
- **TikTok:** Perfect for short-form, viral video content.
- **Descript:** A powerful video editing, transcription, and podcast production tool.

Quick-Start Steps:

1. **Master the Basics:** Learn video production techniques and editing software.

2. **Study Success:** Analyze successful video marketing campaigns to understand what resonates with different audiences.
3. **Build a Portfolio:** Create sample video marketing strategies and mock-ups to show potential clients.
4. **Network and Promote:** Set up profiles on platforms like Upwork or reach out directly to businesses.

Tips for Success:

- **Personalize AI Content:** Use AI tools for initial drafts, but refine scripts and visuals to ensure they align with brand voice and objectives.
- **Hone Your Editing Skills:** Develop a good grasp of video editing and motion graphics to elevate your content.
- **Learn Video SEO:** Optimize your videos for search engines by understanding platform-specific algorithms and using the right keywords.
- **Stay Trendy:** Follow the latest trends in video marketing and experiment with new formats, such as live video or interactive content.

Video marketing is visual storytelling, and with the right blend of AI tools and creative input, you can deliver impactful content that engages audiences and drives results. As you grow your side hustle, consider specializing in certain video types or platforms to hone your niche. Building solid relationships with clients, refining your technical skills, and staying current with trends can ensure long-term success in video marketing.

40. Content Marketing

Do you have a knack for storytelling and enjoy helping brands connect with their audience? Content marketing offers an exciting way to blend creativity with strategy, producing valuable and relevant content that attracts and engages target customers. With AI tools like ChatGPT, you can supercharge your brainstorming sessions, draft initial content, and streamline your content planning. Your value lies in refining these AI-generated ideas into impactful content strategies that build your clients' trust, authority, and engagement.

How to Use AI Tools:

- **Brainstorm Ideas:** Use ChatGPT to generate topics, headlines, and themes for blog posts, whitepapers, and social media.
- **Create Outlines:** Develop content outlines for articles, case studies, or videos to structure your content effectively.
- **Draft Posts:** Quickly generate drafts of social media posts or promotional copy for your content.
- **Plan Distribution:** Generate content calendars and schedule content for consistent platform engagement.

Potential Earnings:

- $15 - $40+ per hour, depending on your work scope and expertise. As your client base grows, you can command higher rates.

Platforms to Use:

- **HubSpot:** For content management and marketing automation.
- **WordPress:** For managing blog content and publishing.
- **CoSchedule:** Ideal for content planning and scheduling across teams.

Quick-Start Steps:

1. **Study Content Strategies:** Analyze successful marketing campaigns to understand what works across different industries.
2. **Learn SEO Fundamentals:** Understanding how search engine optimization integrates with content marketing is crucial for visibility.
3. **Create Sample Plans:** Develop content marketing plans for fictional brands to demonstrate your ability to create a cohesive strategy.
4. **Build a Portfolio:** To attract potential clients, showcase diverse content types such as blog posts, infographics, or video scripts.

Tips for Success:

- **Refine AI Content:** Use AI to generate drafts, but fine-tune each piece to match the brand's voice and provide genuine value.
- **Measure Success:** Develop data analysis skills to track content performance and optimize future campaigns.
- **Understand the Audience:** Learn about buyer personas and map the customer journey to create targeted content.
- **Stay Updated:** Keep up with the latest trends in content marketing, from long-form content to video marketing.

With content marketing, you build relationships with your audience through valuable, informative content. While AI can provide the building blocks, your expertise in creating strategic plans, understanding customer pain points, and driving engagement will set you apart. Specialize in specific industries or content types, develop your distribution skills, and always focus on delivering quality content that aligns with brand goals. Building a portfolio of successful campaigns and keeping up with content trends will help you become a trusted expert.

41. Affiliate Marketing

Do you enjoy sharing great products and want to earn a steady income stream? Affiliate marketing allows you to recommend products or services you love and get paid for every sale through your unique links. With AI tools like ChatGPT, you can generate engaging content, optimize strategies, and discover new product niches. Your value comes from using these AI insights to build trust with your audience and create effective affiliate campaigns that deliver accurate results.

How to Use AI Tools:

- **Generate Product Reviews:** ChatGPT outlines and creates detailed product reviews highlighting key features and benefits.
- **Create Calls-to-Action:** Write persuasive calls-to-action encouraging clicks and driving conversions through affiliate links.
- **Draft Email Sequences:** Create engaging email campaigns for affiliate product promotions.
- **Analyze Product Niches:** Use AI to identify trending products and profitable niches to tap into for affiliate success.

Potential Earnings:

- Highly variable. You could earn $25 - $50 per hour doing affiliate marketing for clients or grow your affiliate business for potentially limitless income.

Platforms to Use:

- **Amazon Associates:** Ideal for a wide range of physical products.
- **ClickBank:** Great for promoting digital products.
- **ShareASale:** Offers access to diverse affiliate programs across multiple industries.

Quick-Start Steps:

1. **Choose a Niche:** Pick a product category that interests you and has strong earning potential.
2. **Set Up Your Platform:** Create a blog, YouTube channel, or social media page to host your affiliate content.
3. **Apply to Affiliate Programs:** Join affiliate networks that align with your chosen niche.
4. **Create a Content Strategy:** Plan out product reviews, comparisons, and how-to guides that naturally incorporate affiliate links.

Tips for Success:

- **Add Personal Insights:** Use AI-generated content as a foundation, but personalize it with your experiences and recommendations.

- **Build Audience Trust:** Focus on creating honest, valuable content that strengthens your relationship with your audience.
- **Master SEO:** Learn search engine optimization to drive organic traffic to your affiliate content.
- **Diversify Income Streams:** Work with multiple affiliate programs to spread risk and increase earning opportunities.

Affiliate marketing thrives on authenticity. AI can help you generate content, but your voice, recommendations, and relationship with your audience are what genuinely make the difference. Promoting products you believe in and creating high-quality content that adds value can build a long-lasting, successful affiliate marketing side hustle. Consider specializing in specific product categories, learning SEO and email marketing, and always staying transparent about your affiliate relationships with your audience. Stay informed on industry trends and refine your strategies to see continuous growth and engagement.

42. Marketing Analytics

Do you love uncovering hidden patterns and using data to shape successful strategies? Marketing analytics could be the perfect side hustle for you! It's all about diving into data to help businesses fine-tune their marketing efforts and boost their ROI. With AI tools like ChatGPT, you can streamline the process by analyzing trends, generating insights, and predicting future performance. Your role is to transform these AI-powered insights into actionable recommendations that drive real marketing success for your clients.

How to Use AI Tools:

- **Interpret Data Patterns:** Use ChatGPT to spot trends and offer possible explanations for marketing results.
- **Generate Report Outlines:** Create clear, data-focused report structures and visual elements for presenting insights.
- **Build Predictive Models:** Use AI to create models based on historical data that can predict future performance.
- **Draft Strategic Recommendations:** Turn data insights into actionable, data-driven marketing strategies for clients.

Potential Earnings:

- $15 - $45 per hour, depending on your work scope and expertise.

Platforms to Use:

- **Google Analytics:** Ideal for tracking website performance and analyzing campaign effectiveness.
- **SEMrush:** Great for SEO and competitor analysis.

- **Tableau:** For powerful data visualization and insights presentation.

Quick-Start Steps:

1. **Learn Marketing Analytics Basics:** Understand key performance indicators (KPIs) and how they reflect marketing success.
2. **Master Data Tools:** Get familiar with platforms like Google Analytics and Tableau for collecting and visualizing data.
3. **Create Sample Reports:** Practice creating marketing analytics reports for hypothetical campaigns to showcase your skills.
4. **Build a Portfolio:** Gather your best work to demonstrate your ability to turn data into valuable insights for potential clients.

Tips for Success:

- **Validate AI-Generated Insights:** Use AI to kickstart the process, but always apply critical thinking to ensure accuracy.
- **Master Data Visualization:** Learn how to present data in easy-to-understand and impactful ways for decision-makers.
- **Stay Current:** Keep up with the latest trends in marketing analytics tools and methodologies.
- **Translate Data into Action:** Develop the skill of turning complex data sets into clear, actionable client recommendations.

Marketing analytics involves translating data into insights that can create a tangible impact. AI can help process the data, but your critical thinking and strategic expertise combine it. Consider specializing in specific types of analytics (like SEO or campaign performance), and always stay mindful of data privacy regulations. You'll build client trust by consistently delivering clear, data-driven recommendations and setting yourself up for long-term success. Stay curious, keep learning, and you'll be ready to tackle the ever-evolving world of marketing analytics!

43. PPC Campaign Management

If you love seeing instant results from your marketing efforts and enjoy the challenge of optimizing campaigns for maximum impact, PPC Campaign Management might be your perfect side hustle! It's all about creating targeted, data-driven paid ads that get accurate results on Google, Facebook, or other ad platforms. With AI tools like ChatGPT, you can streamline campaign creation, keyword selection, and performance analysis to optimize every dollar spent. Your role is to turn these AI-powered insights into high-performing PPC campaigns that deliver impressive ROI for your clients.

How to Use AI Tools:

- **Generate Ad Copy Variations:** Use ChatGPT to create different versions of ad copy for A/B testing.
- **Build Keyword Lists:** Create target and negative keyword lists to optimize ad relevance.
- **Draft Ad Extensions:** Write site links, callouts, and structured snippets to enhance ad performance.
- **Analyze Campaign Data:** Leverage AI to spot trends and suggest optimizations for better results.

Potential Earnings:

- $24 - $60 per hour through platforms, depending on campaign size and your expertise.

Platforms to Use:

- **Google Ads:** For search, display, and shopping ads.
- **Facebook Ads Manager:** For social media advertising.
- **Microsoft Advertising:** Formerly Bing Ads, another valuable platform.
- **Upwork:** Find clients and freelance PPC opportunities.

Quick-Start Steps:

1. **Get Certified:** Obtain certifications in Google Ads and other vital platforms to boost your credibility.
2. **Learn Campaign Types:** Familiarize yourself with search, display, shopping, and video campaigns.
3. **Create Sample Campaigns:** Practice by building PPC campaigns for hypothetical businesses.
4. **Build a Portfolio:** Showcase your results-driven approach with actual or sample campaigns demonstrating your skills.

Tips for Success:

- **Refine AI Outputs:** Use AI-generated ideas as a starting point, but tailor them to each platform's best practices and your client's goals.
- **Master Analytics:** Sharpen your analytical skills to interpret data and adjust campaigns for better performance.
- **Stay Updated:** PPC platforms like Google and Facebook are constantly evolving. Stay up to date with the latest features and updates.
- **Understand Conversion Tracking:** Learn about conversion tracking and attribution to measure your campaign's impact.

PPC Campaign Management is about strategic decision-making, data analysis, and continuously optimizing campaigns for success. AI can help generate ideas and analyze data, but your expertise in targeting, budgeting, and interpreting performance metrics will set you apart. Consider specializing in industries or ad types (e.g., e-commerce, lead generation), and develop skills in cross-channel marketing and conversion rate optimization to expand your services. You'll build trust and secure long-term clients by consistently delivering solid results and managing budgets wisely. Stay competitive by continuously learning and staying on top of PPC trends and best practices!

Digital Products & Services Side Hustles

"Technology is best when it brings people together."

Matt Mullenweg

Digital products and services offer an exciting opportunity to leverage technology and creativity to generate income with minimal overhead. Whether hosting webinars, building membership sites, flipping websites, or developing apps, this side hustle category enables you to tap into the growing demand for online content and digital solutions. With AI tools like ChatGPT, you can streamline content creation, automate tasks, and enhance productivity, allowing you to focus on delivering value and scaling your business. This section explores various ways to harness digital products and services, providing insights into how you can turn your skills into profitable ventures.

44. Webinar Creation

Hosting webinars is a powerful way to share expertise and connect with audiences in real-time. Whether creating or promoting a product or service, you can use AI tools like ChatGPT to generate outlines, script presentations, and brainstorm interactive elements. Imagine using AI to craft a polished webinar while adding your unique touch – this side hustle has endless possibilities! You can host webinars or offer expertise to help others create professional presentations.

Don't forget to jot this one down in your journal! Webinar creation can seamlessly complement many other side hustles, whether launching a product, building a brand, or sharing your expertise. The potential to enhance your projects and connect with audiences is limitless.

How to Use AI Tools:

- **Brainstorm Webinar Topics:** Use ChatGPT to generate ideas based on audience interests or industry trends.
- **Create Detailed Outlines:** Develop structured, informative content for each webinar session.
- **Script Webinar Dialogues:** Draft talking points, transitions, and calls to action with AI assistance.
- **Generate Polls and Q&A Ideas:** Incorporate interactive elements to engage attendees and encourage participation.

Potential Earnings:

- $500 - $3,000+ per webinar, depending on your niche, audience size, and the complexity of the content.

Additionally, if you create webinars for clients, you can charge on a per-project basis or earn consulting fees.

Platforms to Use:

- **Zoom:** Popular for live webinars with interactive features.
- **WebinarJam:** Designed to host professional webinars with marketing tools.
- **Demio:** Known for its user-friendly webinar interface.
- **Teachable:** Ideal for packaging and selling recorded webinars as online courses.
- **Upwork** and **Fiverr:** Perfect platforms to find clients seeking help with webinar creation.
- **LinkedIn:** Great for connecting with businesses and professionals seeking webinar services.

Quick-Start Steps:

1. **Pick a Topic:** Identify a subject you're passionate about or have expertise in.
2. **Research Your Audience:** Understand what interests them and tailor your content accordingly.
3. **Create an Outline:** Use AI to help structure your content flow and talking points.
4. **Set Up a Webinar Platform:** Choose a platform that matches your live streaming and interaction needs.
5. **Offer Webinar Services to Clients:** Reach out to businesses or individuals who could benefit from webinars for training or marketing purposes.

Tips for Success:

- **Use AI as a Foundation:** Start with AI-generated content, then personalize it with your style and expertise.
- **Focus on Engagement:** Include interactive elements like polls and Q&A sessions to keep your audience involved.
- **Promote Your Webinar:** Build an email list and promote your event on social media or through collaborations.
- **Record and Repurpose:** After hosting, consider repurposing the content into an evergreen product or online course.

Creating webinars is a powerful way to connect with your audience and showcase your expertise and a lucrative service you can offer other businesses. While AI tools can assist with content creation and structure, your insights and presentation skills make webinars stand out. Whether writing your own or helping others, webinars are an impactful and flexible side hustle to explore.

45. Membership Site Creation

Building a membership site is an incredible way to share your expertise, create a community, and offer exclusive content. Imagine having your platform where people pay to access your knowledge, resources, or networking opportunities – exciting, right? With AI tools like ChatGPT, you can generate fresh content ideas, craft engagement strategies, and keep your members excited with regular updates. This side hustle might be perfect for you if you want to build a space where people connect, learn, and grow!

Be sure to include this idea in your journal! A membership site could be the perfect complement to other side hustles you're building, offering a platform for your audience to connect, learn, and grow. Imagine the potential of turning your expertise into a thriving community where members keep coming back for more!

How to Use AI Tools:

- **Brainstorm Membership Themes:** Use ChatGPT to generate ideas for your site's theme and focus.
- **Generate Content Outlines:** Plan out regular updates like articles, videos, or podcasts that keep members engaged.
- **Create Engagement Prompts:** Develop conversation starters or activities to foster community interaction.
- **Draft Newsletters:** Keep members informed with AI-generated email newsletters and updates.

Potential Earnings:

- $200 - $15,000+ per month, depending on the number of members, pricing structure, and value provided.

Platforms to Use:

- **Patreon:** Ideal for creators who want to offer tiered memberships.
- **Memberful:** Great for integrating membership features with your existing website.
- **Wild Apricot:** Tailored for associations or clubs managing memberships.
- **Upwork** and **Fiverr:** Perfect for finding clients who need assistance setting up or managing their membership sites.

Quick-Start Steps:

1. **Identify Your Niche:** Choose a focus for your membership site that you're enthusiastic about and has a dedicated audience.
2. **Create Your Value Proposition:** Develop an apparent reason for members to join – what exclusive value are you providing?
3. **Plan Your Content:** Use AI to brainstorm a content calendar to engage members with fresh, valuable updates.

4. **Set Up Your Platform:** Choose the right membership platform for your audience and set up a user-friendly site structure.

Tips for Success:

- **Personalize AI-Generated Ideas:** Start with AI for content ideas but refine based on real-time member feedback and interactions.
- **Consistency is Key:** Regularly provide high-quality content that keeps members engaged and wanting more.
- **Onboard with Care:** Ensure a seamless onboarding process that welcomes new members and highlights the site.
- **Engage and Build Community:** Actively participate in your site's community, gathering feedback and encouraging interaction.

Fostering a vibrant community and offering unique insights are crucial for successful membership sites. Consider introducing tiered memberships or specialized sub-groups as your platform grows, and focus on community management, digital product creation, and retention marketing to enhance success. Uphold ethical standards by prioritizing member values, maintaining transparency, and protecting privacy. Building a thriving membership site takes patience and persistent effort. Focus on cultivating loyalty, engaging with fellow membership site owners, and staying informed about industry trends for valuable insights. Ensure compliance with data protection regulations and create a secure and trustworthy environment for long-term member contributions.

46. Website Flipping

Website flipping is a unique, high-reward side hustle that allows you to combine digital skills with entrepreneurial savvy. Imagine purchasing an undervalued website, improving its content, SEO, and functionality, and selling it for a substantial profit! With AI tools like ChatGPT, you can streamline tasks like content creation and market analysis, making the process more efficient. While this side hustle may not directly align with others, it offers an exciting opportunity to dive deep into digital entrepreneurship and generate significant income from each flip.

How to Use AI Tools:

- **Generate Improvement Ideas:** Use ChatGPT to brainstorm ways to enhance content, design, and user experience.
- **Create New Content:** Boost traffic and SEO with fresh, high-quality articles and posts.
- **Analyze Metrics:** Leverage AI to evaluate traffic, revenue, and audience engagement, then suggest optimizations.
- **Write Sales Descriptions:** Draft compelling copy to attract buyers and showcase your site.

Potential Earnings:

- $500 - $50,000+ per flip, depending on niche, traffic, and revenue growth factors.

Platforms to Use:

- **Flippa:** A popular marketplace for buying and selling websites.
- **Empire Flippers:** Ideal for selling higher-value websites with consistent earnings.
- **Motion Invest:** Great for selling smaller websites or starter projects.

Quick-Start Steps:

- **Learn Website Valuation**: Understand the key metrics like traffic and monetization strategies.
- **Start Small**: Buy an affordable site to practice improving and flipping it.
- **Use AI**: Implement AI tools to enhance content, SEO, and user engagement.
- **Boost Value**: Learn how to increase traffic and revenue through SEO and digital marketing

Tips for Success:

- **Start with AI**: Use AI to generate content ideas but refine them to fit the website.
- **Focus on Metrics**: Pay attention to boosting key performance indicators like traffic, bounce rate, and revenue.
- **Learn Basic Design**: Acquire basic web design or coding skills to improve user experience.
- **Stay Informed**: Keep up with digital marketing trends and SEO techniques to stay competitive.

Website flipping offers a unique path into digital entrepreneurship. While it requires dedication and specific skills, the rewards can be substantial. Use AI to streamline your efforts, but rely on your market knowledge, digital marketing skills, and creativity to maximize your returns.

47. Domain Flipping

Domain flipping is an exciting way to tap into the digital real estate market, where a single, well-chosen domain name can become a lucrative sale. Imagine finding an undervalued domain, purchasing it for a few dollars, and then selling it for thousands! With AI tools like ChatGPT, you can brainstorm domain name ideas, analyze market trends, and craft persuasive sales pitches, making this process more efficient and effective. While it takes a sharp eye and strategic thinking, domain flipping can be a rewarding side hustle for those willing to dive in.

How to Use AI Tools:

- **Brainstorm Domain Names**: Use ChatGPT to generate creative and brandable domain name ideas.
- **Identify Trending Keywords**: Let AI help you find relevant keywords and phrases that can inspire valuable

domain names.

- **Analyze Market Trends**: Research niches and trends to identify potentially high-value domains.
- **Craft Sales Pitches**: Draft compelling descriptions highlighting a domain's potential.

Potential Earnings:

- $100 - $10,000+ per domain, with some premium domains selling for significantly more.

Platforms to Use:

- GoDaddy Auctions: A marketplace for buying and selling domains.
- Namecheap: Popular for finding affordable domains and flipping them.
- Sedo: Ideal for listing premium domains to a global audience.

Quick-Start Steps:

1. **Learn Domain Valuation**: Study factors like length, brandability, and industry relevance.
2. **Start Small**: Buy a few promising domains with a modest budget to test the market.
3. **Leverage AI**: Use AI tools to generate domain ideas and research trends.
4. **List on Marketplaces**: Explore different platforms to sell your domains and develop effective listings.

Tips for Success:

- **Start with AI, Then Refine**: Use AI-generated domain ideas, but trust your instinct to pick names that stand out.
- **Keep it Short and Memorable**: Focus on domain names that are easy to remember and brand.
- **Understand Domain Extensions**: Research the value of extensions like .com, .net, and country-specific ones.
- **Stay Informed**: Follow trends in technology, business, and industry to predict which domains might increase in value.

Domain flipping requires a balance of creativity, market insight, and strategic planning. While AI can assist in generating ideas and analyzing trends, your ability to spot marketable domains and negotiate deals is vital. Specializing in specific niches, such as tech or e-commerce, and learning to market domains effectively will help you stand out. Stay informed about new developments in domain registration and internet trends, and over time, build a portfolio of quality domains that can lead to higher profits.

48. App Development

Imagine transforming a great idea into a fully functioning app that people can download. App development allows you to create mobile or web applications that entertain, solve problems, or make life easier. With AI tools like ChatGPT, you can streamline the entire process – from generating app ideas to designing user interfaces and even tackling basic coding tasks by combining AI's capabilities and your technical expertise; your apps that meet market demand and stand out in today's landscape.

How to Use AI Tools:

- **Brainstorm App Ideas and Features:** Use ChatGPT to generate creative app ideas and must-have features.
- **Create User Stories and App Descriptions:** Define user journeys and draft app descriptions that speak to your audience.
- **Develop Outlines for Documentation:** Create clear, structured user guides and app documentation with AI assistance.
- **Draft Marketing Copy and App Store Descriptions:** Use AI to craft compelling descriptions that attract potential users.

Potential Earnings:

- $25 - $85 per hour on platforms like Upwork, or $1,500 - $44,000+ per month, depending on app popularity and your monetization strategy.

Platforms to Use:

- **Google Play Store:** Ideal for publishing and monetizing Android apps.
- **Apple App Store:** The go-to platform for iOS app distribution and sales.
- **PWA Builder:** A helpful tool for creating and distributing cross-platform web applications.

Quick-Start Steps:

1. **Learn a Programming Language:** Master coding languages like Swift, Kotlin, or JavaScript.
2. **Familiarize Yourself with Development Tools:** Explore frameworks and tools designed for app creation.
3. **Use AI to Design:** Let AI assist with generating app ideas and designing a prototype.
4. **Develop an MVP:** Create a minimum viable product and seek user feedback to refine your app.

Tips for Success:

- **Refine with Market Research:** Use AI-generated ideas as a base, but hone them using insights from market research and user feedback.
- **Focus on User Experience:** Create intuitive apps that offer a seamless user experience.
- **Explore Monetization Strategies:** Learn the ins and outs of app monetization, such as freemium models, subscriptions, or in-app purchases.
- **Stay Updated:** Keep informed about the latest app development trends and best practices.

Developing apps is more than just writing code – solving problems, creating engaging experiences, and constantly improving. You can boost your productivity by leveraging AI tools, but your expertise will set you apart in this competitive market. Specialize in a niche, build a portfolio of unique and functional apps, and consistently improve your skills to stay ahead of the curve.

49. Software Development

Software development offers the opportunity to build solutions that solve real-world problems or meet specific needs. Whether operating systems or standalone programs, AI tools like ChatGPT can assist in generating code, brainstorming solutions, and drafting documentation. Imagine speeding up the coding process while maintaining your creative and technical control – software development is an exciting, limitless side hustle that can become a full-time passion. Plus, the field is continuously evolving, allowing you to stay on the cutting edge of technology!

How to Use AI Tools:

- **Draft Requirements:** Use ChatGPT to help create software specifications and requirement documents.
- **Generate Code Snippets:** Get assistance in generating code or pseudo-code for functionalities.
- **Document Your Software:** Create outlines for user manuals and technical documentation.
- **Solve Complex Problems:** Use AI to brainstorm solutions for tricky coding challenges.

Potential Earnings:

- $10 - $100+ per hour, depending on software complexity and your expertise.

Platforms to Use:

- **GitHub:** Essential for version control and contributing to open-source projects.
- **Stack Overflow:** Join the community to solve problems and share expertise.
- **Upwork** or **Toptal:** Ideal for finding freelance software development jobs.

Quick-Start Steps:

1. **Master Programming Languages:** Start with one or more languages (Python, Java, C++).
2. **Learn Development Methodologies:** Familiarize yourself with Agile, Scrum, or other methods.
3. **Build a Portfolio:** Showcase your projects, possibly using AI to assist with ideation and code generation.
4. **Join Freelance Platforms:** Set up profiles on freelance sites or seek employment at tech companies.

Tips for Success:

- **Review and Optimize AI-Generated Code:** Always refine AI-generated outputs for efficiency and readability.
- **Write Clean Code:** Ensure your code is well-documented, maintainable, and efficient.
- **Stay Updated:** Keep up with the latest programming languages, frameworks, and tools.
- **Enhance Problem-Solving Skills:** Develop your debugging and troubleshooting abilities.

Software development offers boundless possibilities if you're willing to learn and adapt continually. While AI can assist with coding and documentation, your expertise lies in creating functional, reliable, and secure software solutions. Specialize in specific types of software or industries and develop complementary skills like user experience design or cybersecurity. Upholding ethical standards around user privacy and security is crucial in this field. Build a strong portfolio, contribute to open-source projects, and engage with the developer community to grow your reputation and skillset. Stay curious, and you'll thrive in the ever-evolving world of software development.

50. E-commerce Store Creation

Building an online store is more than just putting products on a website – it's about creating a seamless shopping experience that keeps customers returning. Imagine setting up an e-commerce store, from designing the perfect layout to crafting irresistible product descriptions, all while automating tasks like customer service and marketing campaigns with the help of AI tools like ChatGPT. Whether you're building a store for yourself or a client, this side hustle can generate significant income and grow into something much bigger!

How to Use AI Tools:

- **Product Descriptions:** Use ChatGPT to write compelling, SEO-optimized product descriptions.
- **Customer Service:** Automate responses to frequently asked customer questions.
- **Marketing Campaigns:** Draft email marketing campaigns and newsletters with AI-generated content.
- **Sales Strategies:** Generate creative ideas for promotions, discounts, and seasonal sales.

Potential Earnings:

- $3,000 - $10,000+ per store setup, plus potential ongoing management fees or a percentage of sales.

Platforms to Use:

- **Shopify:** For scalable, user-friendly e-commerce solutions.
- **WooCommerce:** Perfect for WordPress-based stores.
- **BigCommerce:** Ideal for larger, more feature-rich online stores.

Quick-Start Steps:

1. **Learn E-commerce Basics:** Familiarize yourself with major e-commerce platforms and online retail strategies.
2. **Master Marketing and SEO:** Understand how to drive traffic and sales using digital marketing and search engine optimization.
3. **Build a Sample Store:** Create a mock store to showcase your skills to potential clients.
4. **Network for Clients:** Reach out to small businesses or use freelance platforms to find clients needing e-commerce solutions.

Tips for Success:

- **Customize AI Content:** Use AI-generated content as a foundation, but personalize it to fit each brand brand and SEO needs.
- **Design User-Friendly Stores:** Ensure smooth navigation, intuitive designs, and seamless checkout processes to enhance user experience.
- **Understand Payment and Shipping Solutions:** Learn about various payment gateways and shipping providers and how they integrate with your store.
- **Stay Updated on Trends:** Follow e-commerce trends, consumer behaviors, and seasonal shopping habits to keep your store competitive.

While AI can streamline content creation and automation tasks, your expertise in e-commerce strategy, customer experience, and product management is essential for long-term success. Focus on specific e-commerce models, such as dropshipping, print-on-demand, or subscription boxes, and refine your skills in inventory management, analytics, and conversion rate optimization. Always maintain ethical standards when handling customer data and providing precise product details. By building a portfolio of successful stores and staying current with market trends, you'll position yourself to attract high-value clients – or perhaps even launch your thriving e-commerce empire!

51. Dropshipping

Imagine running an online store without ever worrying about managing inventory. That's the beauty of dropshipping – you focus on selling, and the supplier handles the shipping! With AI tools like ChatGPT, you can easily research winning products, craft compelling product descriptions, and automate customer communication. It's all about using these AI-driven insights to create a streamlined, profitable dropshipping business.

How to Use AI Tools:

- **Identify Trending Products**: Use ChatGPT to research and uncover trending products in your niche.
- **Write Product Descriptions**: Generate unique, engaging product descriptions and catchy titles.
- **Craft Marketing Copy**: Develop effective social media ads, email campaigns, and sales copy with AI assistance.
- **Automate Customer Responses**: Create automated answers for common customer questions to save time.

Potential Earnings:

- $1,000 - $100,000+ per month, depending on your niche, marketing strategies, and business scale.

Platforms to Use:

- **Shopify:** For building and managing your e-commerce store.
- **AliExpress:** To find affordable products for dropshipping.
- **Oberlo:** A tool that connects Shopify with AliExpress for seamless product importing and order fulfillment.

Quick-Start Steps:

1. **Research a Profitable Niche**: Find a niche that aligns with your interests and has demand.
2. **Set Up Your Store**: Use Shopify to build an appealing, easy-to-navigate online store.
3. **Find Suppliers**: Choose reliable suppliers on platforms like AliExpress and import their products into your store.
4. **Market Your Products**: Develop a marketing plan using social media, Google ads, or influencer collaborations.

Tips for Success:

- **Personalize AI Content**: Use AI-generated descriptions and marketing copy as a foundation but customize them for authenticity and appeal.
- **Prioritize Customer Service**: Excellent service can set you apart and build customer loyalty.

- **Master Targeted Ads**: Learn how to use Facebook, Instagram, and Google ads to drive the right traffic to your store.
- **Stay Current**: Keep an eye on e-commerce trends, market shifts, and customer preferences to stay competitive.

Dropshipping can offer tremendous flexibility and income potential, but it's not a "set it and forget it" business. Your success hinges on selecting the right products, smart marketing, and creating a customer-friendly experience. Use AI to enhance your operations, but always inject your personal brand and strategies into the process. Stay curious, and connect with fellow drop shippers to learn and grow in this dynamic space.

Education & Training Side Hustles

"Education is the most powerful weapon which you can use to change the world."
Nelson Mandela

Education and training side hustles offer an incredible chance to make a meaningful difference by sharing your knowledge and skills. Whether you're dedicated to tutoring, language instruction, music lessons, or career coaching, these opportunities allow you to help others grow and achieve their goals. With AI tools like ChatGPT, you can enhance your efficiency by generating customized lesson plans, practice exercises, and feedback, allowing you to focus on personal connections and guidance driving success. This section explores various education and training side hustles that can turn your expertise into a rewarding, income-generating pursuit.

52. Tutoring

Tutoring can be one of the most fulfilling side hustles out there – helping students grasp challenging concepts and watching their confidence grow is incredibly rewarding. Whether you're tutoring math, language arts, science, or any other subject, AI tools like ChatGPT can be your secret weapon to create engaging lessons and customized learning materials. Imagine offering personalized tutoring sessions beyond expectations, thanks to AI-generated study guides and practice problems. This blend of your teaching expertise and AI assistance can make a difference in your students' success.

How to Use AI Tools:

- **Generate Practice Questions:** Use ChatGPT to create personalized problem sets tailored to your student's needs.
- **Create Study Guides:** Develop focused study guides and lesson plans to simplify complex topics.
- **Explain Concepts Clearly:** Generate student-friendly explanations for complex subjects.
- **Engage with Creative Projects:** Use AI to brainstorm interactive activities that make learning more enjoyable.

Potential Earnings:

- $20 - $40+ per hour, depending on your subject expertise and student level.

Platforms to Use:

- **Wyzant:** Connect with students for both online and in-person sessions
- **Pear Deck Tutor:** Focus on online tutoring across various subjects.
- **Tutor.com:** Offer on-demand tutoring services.
- **Upwork:** Find freelance tutoring opportunities.

Quick-Start Steps:

1. **Identify Your Expertise:** Define the subjects or grade levels you're most comfortable teaching.
2. **Create a Profile:** Highlight your qualifications, teaching style, and approach.
3. **Develop Resources:** Use AI to assist in creating engaging learning materials.
4. **Start Small:** Begin tutoring a few students, collect feedback, and build testimonials.

Tips for Success:

- **Supplement, Don't Replace:** Use AI-generated resources to enhance, but not replace, your personalized instruction.
- **Adapt to Learning Styles:** Tailor your lessons to meet each student's unique needs.
- **Stay Current:** Keep up with curriculum updates and education trends.
- **Clear Communication:** Develop strong communication skills to explain even the most challenging concepts.

Tutoring involves comprehending each student's needs and adjusting your methods to support their learning best. While AI helps streamline lesson planning and content generation, your role in creating meaningful connections and offering tailored support is irreplaceable. As you grow your tutoring side hustle, consider specializing in test preparation, advanced subjects, or online tutoring to expand your reach. Building trust with students and parents through clear communication and measurable progress is critical to developing long-term relationships and a strong reputation. Keep refining your skills, stay passionate about education, and enjoy helping students reach their full potential.

53. Language Teaching

Language teaching is an incredibly fulfilling side hustle that lets you share your passion for communication and culture. Whether you're helping someone master English, Spanish, French, or any other language, the joy of watching your students' confidence grow as they grasp new vocabulary and fluency is priceless. With AI tools like ChatGPT, you can create engaging lessons, design fun practice exercises, and develop real-life conversation scenarios to enhance your teaching. Imagine blending AI-generated materials with your expertise to create interactive, dynamic lessons that make language learning enjoyable and effective for your students.

How to Use AI Tools:

- **Create Conversation Practice:** Use ChatGPT to design dialogues that simulate real-life scenarios.
- **Generate Vocabulary Lists:** Develop tailored vocabulary lists and grammar exercises for different levels.
- **Cultural Context:** Create immersive language lessons with cultural references and scenarios.
- **Personalize Lesson Plans:** Use AI to design customized lessons for each student's proficiency.

Potential Earnings:

- $35 - $60+ per hour, depending on your qualifications and the platform you teach on.

Platforms to Use:

- iTalki connects with students from around the world for one-on-one language lessons.
- **VIPKid:** Teach English to students in China through structured programs.
- **Verbling:** Offer lessons in a wide variety of languages to online learners.
- **Upwork:** Find freelance language teaching opportunities.

Quick-Start Steps:

1. **Determine Your Language:** Choose the language(s) you're fluent in and qualified to teach.
2. **Get Certified:** Consider getting a TEFL or TESOL certification to teach English.
3. **Create a Profile:** Sign up on language teaching platforms and highlight your qualifications.
4. **Develop Lesson Materials:** Use AI to assist in creating structured lessons, activities, and exercises.

Tips for Success:

- **Start with AI, but Personalize:** Use AI-generated content as a foundation, then adapt it to your teaching style and each student's needs.
- **Focus on Interaction:** Build lessons around interactive conversations and practice.
- **Incorporate Culture:** Weave cultural elements into lessons to give context and depth to the language.
- **Stay Updated:** Keep learning about new language teaching methods and tools to enhance your lessons.

Helping students master a new language involves more than just learning grammar and vocabulary; it boosts communication confidence. While AI can help streamline lesson planning and practice exercises, the magic of language learning comes from your personal connection and real-time feedback. Specialize in different age groups or language proficiency levels, and we consider offering specialized courses like business language or conversational fluency. Build strong relationships with students, deliver engaging lessons, and continuously improve your language and teaching skills to provide the best learning experience possible. Your dedication will lead to glowing reviews, repeat students, and a thriving side hustle in language teaching!

54. Music Lessons

Teaching music is more than just showing students how to play an instrument or read sheet music – it is about igniting their passion for music and watching their skills grow over time. Whether you're teaching guitar, piano, vocal techniques, or music theory, helping students develop their talents is incredibly rewarding. With AI tools like ChatGPT, you can enrich this experience by generating practice exercises, creating tailored lesson plans, and breaking down complex music theory into simple, understandable concepts. Imagine combining your musical expertise with AI's abilities to offer personalized, engaging lessons that excite and motivate your students.

How to Use AI Tools:

- **Music Theory Made Simple:** Use ChatGPT to generate easy-to-understand explanations and quizzes for your students.
- **Practice Plans:** Develop goal-setting strategies and practice schedules for your students to stay on track.
- **Clarify Concepts:** Break down complex music theory and instrumental techniques into student-friendly language.
- **Engaging Exercises:** Generate creative ideas for practice drills and activities that make learning fun.

Potential Earnings:

- $50+ per hour, depending on your expertise, instrument, and location.

Platforms to Use:

- **Lessonface:** Great for teaching music lessons online.
- **TakeLessons:** Offers both online and in-person lessons.
- **Upwork** and **Fiverr:** Find freelance music teaching gigs
- **Your Own Website:** Build your brand and attract students directly or partner with local music schools.

Quick-Start Steps:

1. **Identify Your Expertise:** Choose the instrument(s) or musical skills you're most qualified to teach.
2. **Develop a Curriculum:** Create a structured outline for beginners, intermediate, and advanced students.

3. **Create an Online Presence:** Set up profiles on music teaching platforms or launch your website.

4. **Gather Teaching Materials:** Use AI to assist in creating lesson plans, exercises, and practice schedules.

Tips for Success:

- **Enhance with AI:** Use AI-generated resources to supplement, not replace, your expertise.

- **Balance Theory & Fun:** Create a well-rounded curriculum that combines theory with practical playing and enjoyment.

- **Adapt to Each Student:** Personalize your teaching approach to match your students' learning styles and goals.

- **Stay Updated:** Keep up with the latest music education and technology trends to offer cutting-edge lessons.

Music teaching is about more than just the notes -connecting with students, helping them build confidence, and cultivating a lifelong love of music. AI can help with lesson planning and theory explanations, but your real value lies in your ability to inspire and guide your students on their musical journey. Consider specializing in specific genres or techniques and engage with local music communities to build a loyal student base. As you continue honing your teaching skills and staying updated on new trends, you'll become a sought-after music instructor, impacting your students' musical lives.

55. Fitness Coaching

Helping people achieve their health and fitness goals can be incredibly rewarding, and as a fitness coach, you get to be a part of that transformative journey. Imagine using your passion for fitness and AI tools like ChatGPT to design personalized workout routines, meal plans, and motivational messages that keep your clients on track. With AI to assist you in creating content and managing client progress, you can focus on what matters most – guiding and motivating your clients to lead healthier, happier lives.

How to Use AI Tools:

- **Personalized Workouts:** Use ChatGPT to craft varied workout routines tailored to each client's fitness level and goals.

- **Meal Plans:** Generate customized meal plans and recipes that align with your client's nutritional needs.

- **Motivational Content:** Develop daily or weekly motivational messages to inspire and encourage clients.

- **Fitness Education:** Create educational materials about exercise techniques, recovery, and nutrition.

Potential Earnings:

- $30 - $100+ per hour for one-on-one sessions or $100 - $500+ monthly for online coaching programs.

Platforms to Use:

- **Trainerize:** Manage your online fitness clients and track their progress.
- **MyFitnessPal:** Help clients with nutrition tracking and meal plan integration.
- **Instagram** and **YouTube:** Build your fitness brand and attract new clients through content.
- **Upwork:** Find freelance fitness coaching opportunities.

Quick-Start Steps:

1. **Certify Yourself:** Obtain relevant fitness certifications (e.g., NASM, ACE) to build credibility.
2. **Specialize:** Define your coaching philosophy and choose a niche or specialization (e.g., weight loss, strength training).
3. **Build a Portfolio:** Start with friends, family, or volunteer coaching to gather testimonials and success stories.
4. **Create Your Online Presence:** Set up profiles on fitness platforms or launch your website to attract clients.

Tips for Success:

- **Customize Plans:** Use AI-generated ideas as a foundation, then personalize each workout and meal plan for your client's unique needs.
- **Prioritize Sustainability:** Focus on creating long-term, enjoyable routines that clients can stick with.
- **Master Client Motivation:** Learn about behavior change psychology to help clients stay consistent and overcome challenges.
- **Stay Informed:** Keep up with the latest fitness trends and advancements in nutritional science to provide the best guidance.

Fitness coaching goes beyond creating workouts; it's providing personalized support, motivation, and accountability that helps clients build lasting habits. While AI can assist with program creation and progress tracking, your expertise and personal connection are critical to your client's success. Specialize in areas that resonate with you, master the art of online coaching, and engage with your clients on a deeper level. You'll build a thriving fitness coaching business that transforms lives by focusing on ethical practices, staying current in fitness knowledge, and maintaining a solid online presence.

56. Cooking Classes

Imagine sharing your passion for food and transforming someone's kitchen skills through your cooking classes! Whether teaching beginners how to make their first meal or helping food enthusiasts master gourmet techniques, you can bring the joy of cooking to life. With AI tools like ChatGPT, you can streamline the creative process by generating new recipe ideas, structuring lessons, and developing culinary tips that make your classes even more dynamic. Blending your love for food with AI assistance can help you teach more effectively and inspire your students to explore the culinary world.

How to Use AI Tools:

- **Recipe Ideas:** Use ChatGPT to create exciting, unique recipes and variations for your classes.
- **Structured Lessons:** Develop lesson plans tailored to specific cuisines or cooking techniques.
- **Culinary Explanations:** Generate simple explanations for cooking terms and methods to improve student understanding.
- **Class Themes:** Create ideas for themed cooking classes, like baking workshops or international cuisine series.

Potential Earnings:

- $25 - $100+ per hour, depending on your expertise, class size, and location.

Platforms to Use:

- **Skillshare:** Ideal for offering online cooking classes.
- **Cozy Meal:** A platform for hosting both online and in-person cooking experiences.
- **Upwork:** A great place to find clients for custom cooking lessons.
- **Your Website/Local Venues:** Promote your classes at community centers or privately.

Quick-Start Steps:

1. **Define Your Specialties:** Identify the cooking skills you excel at (e.g., Italian cuisine, baking, vegan cooking).
2. **Create Lesson Outlines:** Develop detailed outlines for each class, including recipes and cooking techniques.
3. **Set Up a Kitchen Space:** Choose a dedicated area for teaching, whether at home, in a rented kitchen, or virtually.
4. **Promote Your Classes:** Use online platforms and local advertising to attract students.

Tips for Success:

- **Refine AI Recipes:** Use AI as inspiration, but rely on your culinary skills to perfect each dish.
- **Teach Core Skills:** Focus on essential techniques, like knife handling or flavor balancing, to give students a strong foundation.
- **Prioritize Safety:** Emphasize food safety and kitchen hygiene in every class.
- **Stay Current:** Stay informed about the latest food trends and dietary preferences, such as plant-based cooking or gluten-free options.

Being a successful cooking instructor ignites a love for food in your students and provides them with the skills they need to thrive in the kitchen. While AI can assist with planning and creativity, your hands-on experience, passion, and personal connection will make your classes unforgettable. Consider specializing in a particular cuisine or dietary approach, develop engaging video lessons for virtual learners, and build a strong brand presence through social media and local partnerships. By continuously enhancing your culinary skills and finding ways to engage students, you'll grow your cooking class business and inspire a whole new generation of chefs!

57. Online Art Classes

Sharing your passion for art while helping others discover their creative abilities is a rewarding way to connect with aspiring artists. Whether you're guiding someone through their first painting or introducing advanced techniques, online art classes allow you to inspire a global audience. With AI tools like DALL-E and ChatGPT, you can easily enhance your lessons by generating project ideas, crafting lesson plans, and providing art theory content. Your expertise, combined with these AI resources, helps create a rich and engaging learning experience for your students.

How to Use AI Tools:

- **Generate Visual Inspiration:** Use DALL-E to create visual prompts or ideas for new art projects.
- **Lesson Planning:** Leverage ChatGPT to draft structured lesson plans for techniques, styles, or mediums.
- **Explain Art Concepts:** Create simple, engaging explanations for color theory, composition, and other artistic principles.
- **Create Themed Classes:** Use AI to brainstorm ideas for workshops focused on particular styles, techniques, or themes.

Potential Earnings:

- $20 - $500+ per course, depending on the length, format, and expertise.

Platforms to Use:

- **Skillshare:** Perfect for offering a range of online art classes.
- **Craftsy:** Focus on fine art and craft-based instruction.
- **Local Art Centers/Your Website:** Offer in-person classes or build a custom teaching platform.

Quick-Start Steps:

1. **Define Your Niche:** Identify your artistic specialties (e.g., painting, sculpture, digital art) and target students of specific skill levels.

2. **Plan Your Curriculum:** Develop a series of class outlines, including projects and skill-building exercises.
3. **Prepare Your Space:** Set up a teaching area with the supplies needed to conduct lessons effectively.
4. **Build a Portfolio:** Showcase your work alongside student examples to attract new learners.

Tips for Success:

- **Adapt AI Content:** Use AI-generated ideas as inspiration, but infuse them with your teaching style.
- **Balance Skills & Creativity:** Teach foundational techniques while encouraging students to explore their creative expression.
- **Incorporate Art History:** Include lessons on classic and contemporary art trends to inspire students.
- **Guide and Encourage:** Help students find their voice by providing constructive feedback and fostering experimentation.

Becoming an art instructor sparks inspiration and supports creative growth. While AI can assist with structuring your lessons, your ability to connect with students and guide their artistic journey will make the most significant impact. Consider expanding your offerings to include specialized courses, themed workshops, or even art events that attract a broader audience. The key to success lies in continuously refining your teaching methods, staying connected with the art community, and motivating your students to create with confidence and enthusiasm.

58. Tech Skills Training

Teaching tech skills is advantageous in helping others build valuable knowledge in today's digital world. Whether you're guiding someone through basic computer tasks or allowing them to dive into advanced coding, tech skills training empowers learners to thrive in a tech-driven economy. With AI tools like ChatGPT, you can enhance your lessons by generating coding examples, creating tutorials, and developing practice exercises. These AI-generated resources, combined with your technical expertise, will help create engaging and compelling learning experiences for your students.

How to Use AI Tools:

- **Generate Coding Examples:** Use ChatGPT to create code snippets and programming examples for various languages.
- **Create Step-by-Step Tutorials:** Develop comprehensive tech tutorials for different skill levels.
- **Simplify Complex Concepts:** Break down advanced tech topics into beginner-friendly explanations.
- **Develop Practical Projects:** Generate project ideas that allow students to apply what they've learned in real-world scenarios.

Potential Earnings:

- $20 - $40+ per hour on freelance platforms like **Upwork**, or $100 - $200 per class on platforms like **Udemy**

Platforms to Use:

- **Udemy:** Ideal for creating and selling online tech courses.
- **Codecademy:** Great for interactive coding lessons.
- **LinkedIn Learning:** For professional tech training.
- **Upwork:** A valuable platform for finding freelance tech training gigs.

Quick-Start Steps:

1. **Define Your Expertise:** Identify the tech skills you're most qualified to teach and the audience you want to target.
2. **Develop a Curriculum:** Plan lessons and projects for beginners, intermediates, and advanced learners.
3. **Create Sample Lessons:** Develop a few lessons to showcase your teaching style and content.
4. **Set Up on Platforms:** Create profiles on Udemy, LinkedIn Learning, or your teaching website.

Tips for Success:

- **Personalize AI Content:** Start with AI-generated material and adapt it to your students' learning styles.
- **Focus on Practical Learning:** Ensure your lessons provide hands-on experience and real-world applications.
- **Stay Updated:** Keep up with the latest trends and tools to ensure your training is relevant.
- **Contextualize Skills:** Help students understand how their new skills can be applied in professional or personal projects.

When teaching tech skills, it's essential to break down complex concepts, offer practical troubleshooting guidance, and support students through their learning process. Your expertise in simplifying technology and providing hands-on learning is vital to their success. Specializing in specific tools or industries can help you stand out while creating interactive and engaging learning experiences that motivate your students. Stay current with evolving technologies, maintain high ethical standards, and continue honing your skills to establish yourself as a trusted resource in the tech training field.

59. Life Coaching

Imagine the fulfillment of guiding someone to achieve their personal or professional dreams! Life coaching allows you to empower clients, improve their self-awareness, and inspire them to live more satisfying lives. By leveraging AI tools like ChatGPT, you can supercharge your coaching practice by generating customized growth plans, creating reflective exercises, and crafting motivational content. Your unique coaching approach and AI-generated resources will help you provide impactful, tailored guidance to clients eager for change.

How to Use AI Tools:

- **Formulate Personalized Frameworks:** Use ChatGPT to help create goal-setting strategies tailored to each client's needs.
- **Design Self-Assessment Tools:** Develop reflective prompts and questionnaires that promote personal growth.
- **Create Action Plans:** Generate bespoke plans aligned with each client's aspirations and challenges.
- **Provide Motivation:** Develop daily affirmations and exercises to keep clients inspired.

Potential Earnings:

- $20 - $300+ per hour, or create an online course and make $50 - $200+ per person.

Platforms to Use:

- **BetterUp:** Ideal for professional coaching services.
- **Coach.me:** Focus on goal-setting and habit tracking.
- **Udemy:** Teach others how to become Life Coaches.
- **Your own website or local networking**: Build a personal brand and clientele.

Quick-Start Steps:

1. **Get Certified:** Obtain relevant coaching certifications (e.g., ICF, iPEC).
2. **Define Your Approach:** Establish your coaching philosophy and style.
3. **Build Your Portfolio:** Gather client success stories or offer pro bono sessions to start.
4. **Launch Your Service:** Start on platforms like BetterUp or create your coaching website.

Tips for Success:

- **Personalize AI Content:** Use AI as a foundation, but tailor everything to fit each client's needs and personality.
- **Sharpen Your Skills:** Continue improving your active listening and questioning techniques.
- **Stay Updated:** Keep informed about personal development trends and psychology research.

Being a life coach is about walking alongside your clients as they navigate their path to growth. While AI can provide content and structure, your intuition, empathy, and ability to connect will make all the difference. Consider specializing in career transitions, wellness, or relationships to strengthen your offering. Build trust, foster real connections, and let your passion for helping others shine. Through testimonials and continuous learning, you'll establish yourself as a trusted mentor in life coaching. Engage in continuous professional development and networking to develop yourself as a reliable mentor in life coaching.

60. Career Coaching

Have you ever experienced the satisfaction of helping someone land their dream job or guiding them toward the next giant career leap? Career coaching offers a unique opportunity to impact people's professional lives significantly. Using AI tools like ChatGPT, you can supercharge your career coaching practice by generating tailored career plans, crafting industry-specific resume templates, and developing interview prep materials. You must blend these AI-powered resources with your career expertise to provide clients with strategic, personalized guidance that accelerates their career growth.

How to Use AI Tools:

- **Create Customized Resumes and Cover Letters**: Use ChatGPT to generate industry-specific resume templates and cover letter formats.
- **Build Career Development Plans**: Develop personalized career plans tailored to each client's professional aspirations.
- **Mock Interviews**: Generate mock interview questions and responses for various industries to help clients prepare.
- **Networking and Branding Ideas**: Use AI to brainstorm networking strategies and personal branding content.

Potential Earnings:

- $100 – $150+ per hour for one-on-one coaching, or sell coaching packages for $1,000 - $2,500+.

Platforms to Use:

- **LinkedIn:** Ideal for networking and finding clients.
- **The Muse:** Great for offering career coaching services.
- **Udemy:** Teach others how to become Career Coaches.
- **Your own website or local career centers**: Build a personal brand and attract clients.

Quick-Start Steps:

1. **Get Certified**: Obtain career coaching certifications to enhance your credibility.

2. **Develop Your Methodology**: Establish a coaching methodology with resources tailored to client needs.
3. **Create a Portfolio**: Showcase success stories to build credibility.
4. **Build an Online Presence**: Set up your profiles and network on career platforms and social media.

Tips for Success:

- **Personalize AI Content**: Use AI-generated templates as a base but customize each plan based on the client's goals.
- **Stay Current**: Keep updated on industry trends and job market shifts to provide relevant advice.
- **Expand Your Network**: Build industry connections to offer insider insights and job opportunities.
- **Balance Short and Long-Term**: Focus on both immediate job search tactics and future career advancement strategies.

What sets a career coach apart is the ability to inspire clients to take control of their professional journey and confidently pursue their goals. By blending AI-driven insights with your unique expertise, you can offer transformative guidance that helps clients navigate the complexities of the job market. Whether you specialize in assisting recent grads to break into their fields or guiding seasoned professionals through transitions, your coaching will make a lasting impact. Stay sharp by continuously learning and networking, and establish yourself as a trusted resource in the ever-evolving world of career development.

61. Public Speaking Training

Imagine being the person who helps others conquer their fear of public speaking and deliver powerful presentations that leave lasting impressions. Public speaking training allows you to share your expertise in communication and leadership, empowering clients to present themselves confidently. With AI tools like ChatGPT, you can elevate your coaching by generating customized speech outlines, creating tailored exercises, and developing personalized feedback. Your job is to fuse these AI-generated insights with your experience to guide your clients toward impactful public speaking success.

How to Use AI Tools:

- **Speech Outlines and Ideas**: Use ChatGPT to generate detailed speech outlines and topic suggestions.
- **Customized Exercises**: Create vocal and body language exercises that match each client's unique speaking style.
- **Engagement Techniques**: Develop strategies to help clients connect with their audiences more effectively.
- **Feedback Templates**: Use AI to create constructive feedback frameworks for speech content, delivery, and stage presence.

Potential Earnings:

$25 - $300+ per hour for one-on-one training, or create an online course to earn $50 - $200+ per person.

Platforms to Use:

- **Toastmasters:** Great for networking and finding clients.
- **Udemy:** Ideal for creating and selling online public speaking courses.
- **LinkedIn:** A top platform for landing corporate training gigs.
- **Fiverr:** For side gigs and quick speaking consultation work.

Quick-Start Steps:

1. **Sharpen Your Skills**: Continue honing your public speaking and earn credentials in communication.
2. **Build a Curriculum**: Design a structured training program covering critical public speaking aspects, from confidence to delivery.
3. **Showcase Client Success**: Collect testimonials from clients to demonstrate the effectiveness of your training.
4. **Create an Online Presence**: Use social media and networking platforms to promote your services and connect with clients.

Tips for Success:

- **Customize for Each Client**: Start with AI-generated outlines but tailor the training to fit each client's speaking goals.
- **Confidence and Technique**: Balance confidence-building exercises with technical speaking skills like articulation and timing.
- **Use Video Feedback**: Incorporate video recordings to help clients see their progress and adjust in real-time.
- **Stay Current**: Keep up with the latest presentation technologies and audience engagement strategies.

Helping clients deliver speeches with confidence and clarity is incredibly rewarding. Whether you're coaching executives for corporate presentations or guiding individuals through public speaking fears, your personalized approach and encouragement are essential. Specializing in specific speaking formats—such as TED talks, keynote addresses, or virtual presentations—can further expand your reach. Ethical feedback, continuous self-improvement, and strong industry connections are essential to thriving in this field. By showcasing your expertise and inspiring confidence in your clients, you'll become a go-to public speaking trainer with the power to transform lives through the art of communication.

62. Freelance Writing Coaching

Helping aspiring writers unlock their full potential can be an enriching experience, and freelance writing coaching allows you to guide others toward a fulfilling and successful writing career. Imagine using your writing expertise to inspire, support, and empower others to achieve their goals. With AI tools like ChatGPT, you can enhance your coaching by generating writing prompts, developing personalized improvement plans, and creating marketing strategies. Combining AI-generated insights with your professional know-how allows you to offer coaching that makes a difference in your clients.

How to Use AI Tools:

- **Writing Prompts**: Use ChatGPT to create client exercises and prompts to challenge and develop your client's writing skills.
- **Pitch Templates**: Provide ready-to-use templates for clients to pitch their writing ideas to potential clients.
- **Improvement Plans**: Develop personalized writing improvement plans based on the individual strengths and weaknesses of each client.
- **Niche and Branding Ideas**: Help clients find their unique niche and develop a personal brand using AI to brainstorm ideas and strategies.

Potential Earnings:

- $50 - $100+ per hour for one-on-one coaching, or create an online course and earn $50 - $200+ per person.

Platforms to Use:

- **Udemy** or **Teachable:** Ideal for creating and selling online courses.
- **LinkedIn:** A great place to network and find coaching clients.
- **Your website or blog**: Showcase your coaching expertise and services.

Quick-Start Steps:

1. **Build Credibility**: Highlight your achievements as a successful freelance writer to attract clients.
2. **Create a Curriculum**: Develop a comprehensive coaching program covering essential aspects of freelance writing, such as pitching, finding clients, and improving writing skills.
3. **Prepare Sample Materials**: To enhance your coaching, offer resources like pitch templates, writing tips, and client acquisition strategies.
4. **Establish Your Online Presence**: Create a professional website or blog to promote your coaching services and connect with aspiring writers.

Tips for Success:

- **Tailor AI Content**: Use AI-generated prompts and content as a base, but adapt them to each client's unique goals and style.
- **Focus on Practical Advice**: Provide strategies for finding clients, setting rates, and improving writing.
- **Stay Current**: Stay updated on freelance writing trends, popular niches, and market rates.
- **Mentor Effectively**: Offer a blend of constructive criticism and encouragement to help writers grow in confidence and skill.

Becoming a successful freelance writing coach requires experience and industry insights. While AI tools can support your content and strategy development, your personalized mentorship will make a lasting impact. Specialize in helping writers break into specific niches, from content marketing to creative writing, and consider expanding your coaching to include business skills like client acquisition and digital marketing. Ethical standards, transparency, and a results-driven approach will help you build a reputation as a trusted coach. By staying connected with the industry and continuously honing your craft, you'll inspire and guide the next generation of freelance writers.

Finance & Investment Side Hustles

"An investment in knowledge pays the best interest."

Benjamin Franklin

Finance and investment side hustles offer a unique blend of opportunity and responsibility, helping individuals and businesses navigate complex financial landscapes. Whether deeply interested in investment consulting, cryptocurrency trading, or retirement planning, these side hustles let you blend your expertise with AI tools like ChatGPT to provide personalized, data-driven advice. From crafting tailored strategies to simplifying financial concepts, AI can help streamline your workflow, allowing you to focus on building relationships and delivering value to your clients. Explore this section to discover how to turn your financial knowledge into a rewarding, income-generating side hustle.

63. Investment Consulting

Helping individuals or organizations navigate the complex world of investments can be exciting and rewarding. As an investment consultant, you can guide your clients toward financial success. Imagine combining your expertise with AI tools like ChatGPT to analyze markets, create tailored investment strategies, and simplify financial concepts. With these AI-driven resources, you can elevate your services and offer personalized, data-driven investment advice that sets your clients on a path to wealth building.

How to Use AI Tools:

- **Market Analysis**: Use ChatGPT to evaluate market trends and generate actionable insights for your clients.
- **Investment Strategy**: Create customized strategy templates based on each client's financial goals and risk tolerance.
- **Risk Assessment**: Develop detailed questionnaires and frameworks to help assess risk levels and align investment portfolios accordingly.
- **Simplified Financial Concepts**: Use AI to generate easy-to-understand explanations of complex investment vehicles and strategies.

Potential Earnings:

- $28 - $100+ per hour, depending on your expertise and client portfolio size.

Platforms to Use:

- **E*TRADE:** Access advanced investment tools and research.
- **Bloomberg Terminal:** For comprehensive financial data and in-depth analysis.
- **LinkedIn:** Ideal for networking and connecting with high-net-worth clients.
- **Upwork:** Great for finding freelance clients in need of investment consulting.

Quick-Start Steps:

1. **Earn Certifications**: Obtain the necessary qualifications, such as CFA (Chartered Financial Analyst) or CFP (Certified Financial Planner).
2. **Master Investment Strategies**: Develop a deep knowledge of stocks, bonds, mutual funds, real estate, and other investment vehicles.
3. **Create Sample Portfolios**: Showcase your expertise by building sample portfolios with straightforward strategies.
4. **Network for Clients**: Build relationships with potential clients, financial advisors, and industry professionals for referrals.

Tips for Success:

- **Leverage AI Insights**: Start with AI-generated market insights, then personalize them based on each client's unique needs and financial goals.
- **Stay Informed**: Stay current on economic trends, market movements, and regulatory changes to offer relevant, up-to-date advice.
- **Simplify the Complex**: Develop strong communication skills to explain intricate financial strategies.
- **Build Trust**: Focus on long-term relationships by prioritizing transparency, performance, and client trust.

When providing investment consulting, your role as a trusted advisor is paramount. AI can support your data analysis and help streamline research, but your financial expertise and ability to personalize strategies will make all the difference. To stand out, consider specializing in niche markets, such as socially responsible investing or retirement planning. Upholding ethical practices, ensuring confidentiality, and delivering results-driven guidance will help you build a solid reputation and attract high-value clients. Stay engaged with the ever-changing financial landscape to offer your clients the best possible outcomes.

64. Cryptocurrency Trading Consulting

Diving into the cryptocurrency world can be both thrilling and overwhelming, and that's where cryptocurrency trading consulting shines. Suppose you have a strong interest in helping others navigate the volatile waters of digital currencies. In that case, this side hustle keeps you on the cutting edge of finance and allows you to guide clients through their crypto journeys. By leveraging AI tools like ChatGPT, you can elevate your consulting by creating insightful market analyses, crafting personalized trading strategies, and designing effective risk management frameworks. It would be best to blend AI-driven insights with your crypto expertise to offer informed, real-time advice that leads to smarter trading decisions.

How to Use AI Tools:

- **Market Trend Analysis**: Use ChatGPT to analyze cryptocurrency market trends and generate actionable trading insights.
- **Strategy Templates**: Create personalized trading strategies based on your client's risk tolerance and investment goals.
- **Educational Content**: Develop easy-to-understand guides on blockchain technology and cryptocurrency fundamentals.
- **Scenario Analysis**: Generate scenario analyses to help clients navigate different market conditions and plan accordingly.

Potential Earnings:

- $50 - $500+ per hour, depending on your expertise and the size of your clients' portfolios.

Platforms to Use:

- **CoinGecko** or **CoinMarketCap:** This is for accessing comprehensive cryptocurrency data and analysis.
- **TradingView:** Ideal for technical analysis and charting.
- **Telegram** or **Discord:** For building communities and maintaining client communication.
- **Upwork:** This is for finding clients and managing your freelance business.

Quick-Start Steps:

1. **Master Blockchain & Cryptos**: Develop a deep understanding of blockchain technology and the various cryptocurrencies available.
2. **Build a Track Record**: Start by creating a track record of successful trades, even if it's through paper trading to build credibility.
3. **Create Educational Materials**: Develop easy-to-follow guides and trading strategies that showcase your expertise.
4. **Network & Engage**: Build a network by engaging in crypto forums and social media platforms and attending meetups.

Tips for Success:

- **Use AI as a Springboard**: Let AI-generated insights guide your analysis, but rely on your expertise to make critical decisions in the volatile crypto landscape.
- **Stay Updated**: Continuously monitor new developments in blockchain technology, regulatory changes, and market sentiment.
- **Emphasize Risk Management**: In the unpredictable crypto market, help clients manage risk effectively to safeguard their investments.
- **Balance Analysis Approaches**: Develop expertise in both technical and fundamental analysis for a well-rounded approach to crypto trading.

While AI can provide incredible insights and streamline your work, your knowledge of the crypto market and ability to navigate its volatility will set you apart. Focusing on niche areas of cryptocurrency, developing strong client relationships, and providing clear, research-based advice will help you succeed in this fast-paced world. By staying at the forefront of blockchain advancements and maintaining transparency, you'll build a reputation for offering reliable, cutting-edge consulting.

65. Stock Trading Education

Stock trading education empowers others to understand the financial markets and make informed decisions. If you have a keen interest in stock trading and enjoy helping others succeed, this could be your perfect side hustle. With the help of AI tools like ChatGPT, you can elevate your teaching by generating market analyses, creating strategy templates, and developing engaging, interactive learning materials. You aim to combine these AI-driven resources with your trading expertise to provide practical, real-world knowledge that helps your students succeed.

How to Use AI Tools:

- **Market Concept Explanations**: Use ChatGPT to simplify and explain complex stock market terms and concepts.
- **Trading Plans**: Create personalized templates for trading plans that cater to different investment styles and goals.
- **Scenario-Based Learning**: Develop exercises that simulate various market conditions to prepare students for real-world trading.
- **Stock Screening**: Generate ideas for effective stock screening criteria and technical analysis indicators.

Potential Earnings:

- $50 - $500+ per hour for personalized coaching or $25 - $150+ per person for online courses and workshops.

Platforms to Use:

- **Udemy** or **Coursera:** Ideal for hosting structured online trading courses.
- **Schwab** or **E*TRADE:** For creating demo accounts with access to real-time market data.
- **YouTube:** Share free educational content that builds your brand and attracts students.

Quick-Start Steps:

1. **Create a Curriculum**: Develop a step-by-step curriculum that covers everything from stock market fundamentals to advanced trading strategies.
2. **Sample Portfolios**: Design sample portfolios and strategy documents to illustrate real-world applications.
3. **Engaging Content**: Develop educational content like webinars, videos, and e-books to keep students engaged and motivated.
4. **Build a Presence**: Get involved in finance forums and use social media to attract students and showcase your expertise.

Tips for Success:

- **Enrich AI Content**: Use AI-generated content as a base, but add your insights and experiences to make the lessons more relatable.
- **Risk Management Focus**: Make sure to emphasize risk management techniques as an essential part of any trading strategy.
- **Stay Informed**: Keep up with market trends, regulatory changes, and economic factors that can impact the stock market.
- **Simulated Trading**: Provide hands-on learning through demo accounts or simulated trading environments for practical experience.

Stock trading education is more than technical knowledge – instilling confidence, discipline, and an understanding of market psychology. AI tools can enhance the learning experience; your expertise, practical insights, and real-world experience will resonate with students. Consider specializing in niche trading styles or focusing on specific market sectors. You can become a trusted educator in stock trading by being transparent about risks, avoiding unrealistic promises, and building a reputation for helping students achieve their goals. Regularly engaging your audience with up-to-date market insights, live sessions, or blog content will keep your students informed and eager to learn.

66. Real Estate Consulting

Real estate consulting guides clients through the complex world of property investments, market trends, and management strategies. If you enjoy helping others make informed, data-driven decisions in real estate, this could be the perfect avenue for you. By incorporating AI tools like ChatGPT into your process, you can streamline market analysis, build customized investment strategies, and develop property valuation models. Your expertise and AI-generated insights will empower your clients to confidently navigate the real estate market.

How to Use AI Tools:

- **Market Trend Analysis**: Use ChatGPT to evaluate market trends and identify profitable investment opportunities.
- **Investment Strategies**: Develop personalized strategies for clients based on their financial goals and risk tolerance.
- **Property Valuations**: Create models that assess property values and forecast cash flow for potential investments.
- **Client Reports**: Generate comprehensive market reports and presentation materials to inform clients.

Potential Earnings:

- $36 - $70+ per hour, depending on your expertise and scope of work. A commission-based structure can increase your earnings even further.

Platforms to Use:

- **Zillow** or **Redfin:** Excellent resources for property data and market trends.
- **CoStar:** Provides detailed analytics for commercial real estate.
- **LinkedIn:** Ideal for networking and connecting with potential clients.

Quick-Start Steps:

1. **Get Certified**: Obtain necessary real estate certifications or licenses.
2. **Study the Market**: Thoroughly understand local and national real estate markets.
3. **Create Reports**: Develop sample investment analyses and property evaluation reports to showcase your skills.
4. **Network**: Build relationships with real estate professionals, investors, and potential clients.

Tips for Success:

- **Leverage AI, but Add Expertise**: Start with AI-generated insights and then enhance them with your local market knowledge.
- **Stay Current**: Continuously update your knowledge of real estate laws, market trends, and economic conditions.
- **Simplify Complex Information**: Develop the skill to explain intricate real estate concepts in simple terms for clients.

- **Provide Actionable Advice**: Focus on offering clients clear, practical steps to achieve their investment goals.

In real estate consulting, your ability to interpret data and apply it to the specific needs of your clients will set you apart. AI tools can help with data generation and analysis, but your personalized guidance and deep market understanding are essential for client success. Whether you specialize in residential or commercial real estate, focus on property development, or offer portfolio optimization services, building a reputation for ethical practices and confidentiality will earn your client's trust. Stay engaged with industry professionals, create content to share your knowledge, and continue refining your skills to ensure you remain a sought-after expert in the dynamic world of real estate.

67. Tax Preparation Services

Tax preparation services are all about helping individuals and businesses navigate the often overwhelming world of taxes. If you have a knack for numbers and enjoy helping people navigate their tax obligations, this could be your perfect side hustle. With AI tools like ChatGPT, you can make the process even more efficient by generating clear explanations of tax laws, creating personalized checklists, and developing tax-saving strategies. Pair your tax expertise with AI to offer clients a streamlined, accurate, and stress-free tax filing experience.

How to Use AI Tools:

- **Tax Law Explanations**: Use ChatGPT to simplify and explain complex tax laws and regulations for your clients.
- **Customized Checklists**: Create tailored checklists for different types of taxpayers (e.g., freelancers and small business owners).
- **Tax Templates**: Develop templates for standard deductions and tax situations, saving time on repetitive tasks.
- **Tax-Saving Strategies**: Generate potential tax-saving ideas based on individual or business profiles to maximize client returns.

Potential Earnings:

- $100 - $200+ per tax return, depending on the complexity and experience level.

Platforms to Use:

- **TurboTax ProConnect:** A powerful tool for professional tax preparation.
- **Drake Software:** Provides comprehensive tax planning and preparation.
- **LinkedIn:** Great for networking and finding clients in need of tax services.

Quick-Start Steps:

1. **Get Certified**: Obtain necessary certifications like Enrolled Agent (EA) or Certified Public Accountant (CPA).

2. **Stay Informed**: Regularly update your knowledge of current tax laws and IRS regulations.

3. **Organize Your System**: Create a system to manage and securely store client data.

4. **Educate Clients**: Develop resources to help clients understand their tax responsibilities and savings options.

Tips for Success:

- **AI-Assisted, Human Expertise**: Start with AI-generated content, then tailor your services to each client's tax situation.

- **Accuracy is Key**: Ensure all tax returns are accurate and thorough, focusing on detail.

- **Clear Communication**: Break down complex tax concepts into easily understandable terms for your clients.

- **Stay Ahead of Changes**: Stay current with the latest changes in tax laws, deductions, and credits to provide the best advice.

AI can help you streamline your workflow, but your value as a tax professional lies in your ability to interpret tax laws, identify deductions, and ensure compliance with IRS regulations. Specializing in niche areas such as small business taxes or taxes for freelancers can set you apart. Maintaining strong ethical standards, ensuring client confidentiality, and providing exceptional service are critical to building trust. Continuously staying informed about changes in tax legislation will allow you to offer the most up-to-date advice, helping your clients save money and stay compliant year after year.

68. Financial Planning

Financial planning is helping people make informed decisions to secure their financial futures, whether it's budgeting for the short term or planning for retirement. If you're enthusiastic about assisting others to navigate their finances and achieve their goals, this could be the perfect opportunity for you. With AI tools like ChatGPT, you can streamline your process by creating personalized financial strategies, budgeting templates, and retirement models. The combination of AI-generated insights and your financial expertise allows you to offer clients tailored, actionable advice that helps them take control of their financial future.

How to Use AI Tools:

- **Goal-Setting Frameworks**: Use ChatGPT to generate frameworks for clients to establish and prioritize financial goals.

- **Budget Templates**: Create customized budgets tailored to individual incomes, lifestyles, and financial objectives.

- **Retirement Scenarios**: Develop personalized retirement models and investment strategies based on age, goals, and risk tolerance.

- **Simplify Financial Concepts**: Generate easy-to-understand explanations of complex financial products and investment strategies.

Potential Earnings:

- $35 - 50+ per hour, with the potential for more based on comprehensive financial plans and the complexity of the client's economic situation.

Platforms to Use:

- **Mint** or **YNAB:** This is used to help clients track budgets and manage expenses.
- **Financial Planning Association:** A resource for networking and professional development.
- **LinkedIn:** Ideal for networking and finding high-net-worth clients.
- **Upwork:** This is for finding freelance financial planning clients.

Quick-Start Steps:

1. **Certify Yourself**: Obtain necessary certifications such as CFP (Certified Financial Planner) or ChFC (Chartered Financial Consultant).
2. **Understand Financial Products**: Gain a deep understanding of various financial products and strategies.
3. **Create Sample Plans**: Develop example financial plans and portfolios to showcase your skills.
4. **Network**: Build relationships with potential clients, accountants, and other professionals for referrals.

Tips for Success:

- **Tailored Advice**: Start with AI-generated plans, but always customize them based on each client's financial circumstances and goals.
- **Stay Informed**: Keep up-to-date on tax laws, investment products, and economic shifts.
- **Client Trust**: Build strong relationships by emphasizing transparency and educating clients on their options.
- **Client Empowerment**: Help clients understand the reasoning behind your strategies, empowering them to make informed financial decisions.

The role of a financial planner is much more than numbers – it's about building trust and offering personalized, insightful advice that helps people achieve their financial dreams. AI tools can streamline processes like budget creation and retirement planning, but the real impact comes from your ability to connect with clients and guide them through life's financial challenges. Specializing in areas like estate planning or working with specific client demographics can help you stand out. Always maintain high ethical standards, ensure client confidentiality, and continue educating yourself on emerging financial trends to stay at the top of your field.

69. Crowdfunding Consulting

Crowdfunding can be a powerful tool for turning ideas into reality, but running a successful campaign requires strategy, creativity, and expertise. Crowdfunding consulting could be the perfect side hustle if you're driven by supporting others in reaching their goals. With AI tools like ChatGPT, you can streamline the process by generating innovative campaign ideas, crafting compelling pitches, and developing targeted marketing strategies. Combining these AI-driven insights with your knowledge of crowdfunding can make all the difference in helping clients hit their funding goals and build excitement around their projects.

How to Use AI Tools:

- **Brainstorm Campaign Angles**: Use ChatGPT to create creative rewards, campaign themes, or angles that stand out to backers.
- **Craft Compelling Pitches**: Generate templates for campaign descriptions, updates, and thank-you messages that build a connection with the audience.
- **Plan Video Scripts**: Craft dynamic and engaging pitch videos that fully capture and convey the project's essence.
- **Promotional Strategies**: Develop social media and email marketing strategies tailored to generate buzz and drive traffic to the campaign.

Potential Earnings:

- $50 - $200+ per hour, depending on the project's complexity and your experience level.

Platforms to Use:

- **Kickstarter:** Best for creative and innovative projects.
- **Indiegogo:** A versatile platform for a wide range of campaigns.
- **GoFundMe:** Focused on personal and charitable fundraising.
- **Upwork:** This is for finding clients looking for crowdfunding consultants.

Quick-Start Steps:

1. **Research Successful Campaigns**: Learn from campaigns that have hit their goals and analyze what made them stand out.
2. **Understand Regulations**: Familiarize yourself with crowdfunding regulations and platform rules.
3. **Build a Portfolio**: Create sample campaign materials (e.g., descriptions, videos, marketing strategies) to showcase your skills.

4. **Network in Target Industries**: Build relationships with creators, startups, and industry professionals needing your expertise.

Tips for Success:

- **Tailor AI Content**: Start with AI-generated content but personalize it to align with the client's brand and message.
- **Focus on Storytelling**: Craft engaging narratives that resonate emotionally with potential backers and create a sense of urgency.
- **Stay Current**: Keep up with the latest crowdfunding trends, platform features, and success stories to provide relevant advice.
- **Master Marketing**: Hone your digital marketing skills to drive traffic and engagement across social media, email, and other platforms.

Crowdfunding is an exciting, fast-paced world where creativity and strategic thinking are crucial. AI tools can assist with content creation and campaign planning, but your expertise in building relationships, telling compelling stories, and effectively marketing makes campaigns successful. Consider specializing in specific industries, such as tech, nonprofit, or the arts, to build a niche and attract more clients. Staying on top of platform changes, legal considerations, and evolving marketing trends will ensure your consulting services remain valuable and impactful.

70. Insurance Consulting

Helping individuals and businesses navigate the complex insurance world is rewarding and vital. Insurance consulting could be your perfect side hustle if you enjoy simplifying complicated information and ensuring people are well-protected. By incorporating AI tools like ChatGPT, you can streamline your services by creating risk assessments, comparing policies, and developing tailored strategies that make insurance decisions more accessible for your clients. Leveraging AI, paired with your expertise, allows you to provide data-driven, actionable advice that your clients will trust and value.

How to Use AI Tools:

- **Risk Assessments**: Use ChatGPT to generate questionnaires that assess clients' unique risks and coverage needs.
- **Policy Comparisons**: Create comparison charts to help clients quickly evaluate various insurance providers and product options.
- **Clarifying Policy Terms**: Develop easy-to-understand explanations of complicated insurance clauses, ensuring clients know exactly what they're signing up for.
- **Personalized Strategy**: Generate insurance recommendations based on each client's profile, helping them optimize coverage and minimize risks.

Potential Earnings:

- $20-$45 per hour, depending on the complexity of the consultation and client needs.

Platforms to Use:

- **Policygenius:** A valuable tool for insurance comparisons and market insights.
- **LinkedIn:** Great for professional networking and connecting with potential clients.
- **Upwork:** Ideal for offering freelance insurance consulting services.
- **Industry Forums and Associations**: These can help you stay informed and connect with professionals in the field.

Quick-Start Steps:

1. **Get Certified**: Obtain the necessary insurance licenses and certifications to provide professional advice.
2. **Master the Products**: Develop a deep understanding of various insurance products, from life insurance to commercial policies.
3. **Build a Portfolio**: Create sample insurance policy reviews and risk assessments to demonstrate your expertise.
4. **Network**: Connect with insurance providers, join industry associations, and build a client base through referrals or online platforms.

Tips for Success:

- **Tailor Advice**: Start with AI-generated insights, but customize your advice to meet each client's unique needs.
- **Stay Informed**: Keep up with regulatory changes, industry trends, and new insurance products to provide the best advice.
- **Educate Clients**: Focus on breaking down complex concepts so clients feel empowered in their decisions.
- **Develop Strong Analytical Skills**: Learn to assess risks and coverage effectively to offer valuable, data-driven recommendations.

AI can help streamline risk assessments and policy comparisons, but remember that your expertise will genuinely impact your clients' lives. Specializing in areas like life insurance, health insurance, or corporate policies can set you apart and allow you to serve niche markets. Ethical considerations, such as client confidentiality and avoiding conflicts of interest, are critical in building trust. As you build a reputation for thorough, reliable advice, networking and creating educational materials can further establish your credibility in the insurance world.

71. Debt Management Consulting

Helping people regain control of their finances is incredibly fulfilling. If you enjoy guiding others through challenging financial situations, debt management consulting could perfectly fit you. By integrating AI tools like ChatGPT, you can enhance your debt management services, making the process more efficient and personalized for each client. Whether creating tailored debt reduction strategies or developing easy-to-follow budget templates, combining AI with your financial expertise allows you to provide clear, actionable plans that will make a meaningful difference in your client's lives.

How to Use AI Tools:

- **Generate Debt Reduction Strategies:** Use ChatGPT to create personalized debt repayment plans based on each client's financial situation.
- **Budget Templates:** Create tailored budgeting tools and expense-tracking systems to help clients manage their finances.
- **Debt Management Explanations:** Develop clear explanations of different debt relief options like consolidation, negotiation, or settlement.
- **Customized Action Plans:** Generate step-by-step repayment strategies to help clients stay on track with their debt reduction goals.

Potential Earnings:

- $50 - $300+ per hour, depending on experience and client needs.

Platforms to Use:

- **Credit Karma:** This is used to monitor credit scores and compare financial products.
- **Mint:** Ideal for creating budgeting tools and tracking expenses.
- **LinkedIn:** Great for networking and attracting clients.
- **Upwork:** A platform to find clients looking for financial help.

Quick-Start Steps:

1. **Master Debt Management Strategies:** Learn debt reduction tactics and consumer credit laws.
2. **Create Sample Plans:** Develop example debt reduction strategies and financial analyses to show prospective clients.
3. **Build Industry Relationships:** Partner with credit counseling agencies and financial institutions to create referral networks.
4. **Establish Your Online Presence:** Share educational content on debt management through your website or social media platforms.

Tips for Success:

- **Tailor AI Content:** Use AI-generated content as a starting point, then refine it to match each client's financial situation and goals.
- **Stay Informed:** Keep up with changes in credit laws, debt relief options, and new financial products.
- **Empathy is Key:** Build strong relationships through clear communication and compassion, especially with distressed clients.
- **Provide Actionable Guidance:** Focus on giving step-by-step plans that clients can follow to reduce and manage debt.

Using AI tools to simplify financial calculations and create debt repayment plans can save you time, but your real value comes from your ability to offer empathetic, tailored advice. Specializing in specific types of debt, such as student loans or business debt, can set you apart. Building a solid reputation through successful debt management outcomes and networking with financial professionals will boost your credibility. Always stay updated with the latest trends, laws, and best practices in debt management to offer the most effective solutions to your clients.

72. Retirement Planning

Preparing clients for a secure and fulfilling retirement is understanding their dreams for the future. If you enjoy helping people plan for their post-work lives, retirement planning might be your perfect side hustle. By combining your financial expertise with AI tools like ChatGPT, you can streamline retirement savings projections, craft investment strategies, and create personalized lifestyle plans that align with each client's vision of their golden years. It's all about guiding people toward the future they've always imagined with financial peace of mind.

How to Use AI Tools:

- **Personalized Savings Goals:** Use ChatGPT to calculate retirement savings targets based on client income, lifestyle goals, and timeline.
- **Investment Allocation Models:** Develop customized portfolio strategies tailored to risk tolerance and investment horizon.
- **Lifestyle Questionnaires:** Create retirement lifestyle assessments to help clients plan for leisure, healthcare, and long-term expenses.
- **Retirement Account Explanations:** Generate clear, easy-to-understand information about 401(k)s, IRAs, annuities, and other retirement savings vehicles.

Potential Earnings:

- $50 - $100+ per hour, depending on experience and the complexity of the retirement plan.

Platforms to Use:

- **Vanguard:** Manage retirement accounts and access investment tools.
- **Social Security Administration:** For accurate benefits calculations.
- **Financial Planning Association:** Networking and resources for financial professionals.
- **Upwork:** A platform for finding clients seeking retirement planning services.

Quick-Start Steps:

1. **Get Certified:** Obtain certifications like Certified Financial Planner (CFP) or Retirement Income Certified Professional (RICP).
2. **Master Retirement Accounts:** Deepen your knowledge of retirement savings options, investment strategies, and tax planning.
3. **Create Sample Plans:** Develop example retirement plans and portfolios to showcase your skills.
4. **Network Strategically:** Build relationships with HR professionals, financial advisors, and other referral sources.

Tips for Success:

- **Tailor AI Insights:** Start with AI-generated calculations, then personalize each plan to match your client's financial situation and retirement goals.
- **Stay Informed:** Keep up with changes in retirement regulations, tax laws, and emerging investment opportunities.
- **Communicate with Compassion:** Approach sensitive subjects like healthcare costs and life expectancy with care and empathy.
- **Educate and Empower:** Focus on helping clients understand the value of early planning and consistent savings strategies.

Retirement planning is helping clients envision the next phase of their lives confidently. AI tools can assist in creating data-driven strategies, but your personalized approach and deep understanding of individual needs will set you apart. Consider specializing in unique retirement situations, such as those for business owners or early retirees. Maintain transparency, always act in your client's best interests, and keep learning to provide the best possible advice. With a strong reputation for reliability and success, you'll attract clients who trust you with their financial future.

Customer Service Side Hustles

"Your most unhappy customers are your greatest source of learning."

Bill Gates

The world of customer service has evolved, offering numerous opportunities for flexible and rewarding side hustles. Whether you're interested in virtual customer service, social media support, or implementing customer service software, there's a role that allows you to connect with people and help resolve their issues. With the help of AI tools like ChatGPT, you can streamline your work, create personalized responses, and improve customer experiences, all while working from home or on a freelance basis. Explore this section to find the customer service side hustle that best fits your skills and passion for helping others.

73. Virtual Customer Service Representative

Helping people resolve their issues and providing top-notch support from your home is rewarding and flexible. If you enjoy interacting with others and solving problems, being a virtual customer service representative could be your ideal side hustle. With AI tools like ChatGPT, you can quickly streamline your responses, troubleshoot product issues, and craft polished customer scripts. But your human touch sets you apart – delivering empathetic, personalized service to each customer while leveraging AI for efficiency.

How to Use AI Tools:

- **Response Templates:** Use ChatGPT to quickly draft templates for common inquiries and tailor them to each customer.
- **Troubleshooting Guides:** Create clear, step-by-step instructions to resolve product or service issues.
- **Personalized Interaction:** Generate friendly, professional greetings and closing statements for a customized touch.
- **FAQs:** Develop a comprehensive list of frequently asked questions with clear, concise answers for quick reference.

Potential Earnings:

- $10 - $19+ per hour, depending on the company, the complexity of the issues handled, and your expertise.

Platforms to Use:

- **Zendesk:** Manage customer service tickets and inquiries efficiently.
- **LiveChat:** Provide real-time chat support for immediate customer assistance.
- **Salesforce Service Cloud:** A robust platform for managing all customer service interactions.
- **Upwork:** Find freelance customer service opportunities.

Quick-Start Steps:

1. **Hone Your Skills:** Develop strong communication and problem-solving skills to excel in customer interactions.
2. **Learn the Tools:** Get comfortable with commonly used customer service software and platforms.
3. **Set Up for Success:** Create a quiet, distraction-free workspace with reliable internet access.
4. **Apply for Jobs:** Seek remote customer service roles or freelance positions to start building your experience.

Tips for Success:

- **Start with AI:** Use AI-generated responses as a base, then personalize each to make customers feel valued and understood.
- **Know Your Product:** Become an expert on the product or service you support to provide accurate, helpful advice.
- **Be Empathetic:** Practice active listening and show empathy in every interaction to build customer rapport.
- **Stay Professional:** Maintain calm, even when dealing with demanding or frustrated customers.

Using AI tools in virtual customer service is a great way to increase your efficiency, but the heart of this role is the human connection you build with customers. Personalized service and clear, accurate information are key to success. Specializing in specific industries or mastering certain customer service platforms can boost your side hustle potential. Building a solid reputation for delivering excellent customer care will lead to better opportunities and attract higher-paying clients if you decide to freelance. You may even transition into customer service management or consulting roles as you develop your skills.

74. Customer Experience Consulting

Helping businesses create unforgettable customer experiences is crafting meaningful interactions that foster loyalty and long-term success. If you love customer behavior and delivering top-tier service, customer experience (CX) consulting might be your perfect avenue. With AI tools like ChatGPT, you can take your CX consulting to the next level by generating actionable insights, developing tailored improvement strategies, and creating customer journey maps. Your expertise, combined with AI, allows you to transform businesses by helping them connect with their customers more effectively.

How to Use AI Tools:

- **Customer Personas:** Use ChatGPT to generate detailed customer persona templates, helping businesses understand their target audience.
- **Journey Mapping:** Create comprehensive customer journey maps highlighting pain points and improvement opportunities.
- **Surveys & Feedback:** Develop effective survey questions and frameworks to gather and analyze customer feedback.
- **CX Strategies:** Generate ideas for improving customer experience strategies, from communication practices to loyalty programs.

Potential Earnings:

- $14 - $80+ per hour, depending on your experience and the complexity of the consulting project.

Platforms to Use:

- Qualtrics or SurveyMonkey: This is used to collect and analyze customer feedback.
- Miro: For creating visual customer journey maps.
- LinkedIn: This is for networking with potential clients and showcasing your expertise.

Quick-Start Steps:

1. **Learn CX Fundamentals:** Build a solid foundation in CX principles, customer psychology, and industry best practices.
2. **Create Sample Reports:** Develop sample CX audit reports and strategies to demonstrate your skills.
3. **Build a Portfolio:** Use case studies from actual projects or hypothetical scenarios to showcase your expertise.
4. **Network:** Connect with business owners, marketing professionals, and customer service managers to find potential clients.

Tips for Success:

- **Start with AI:** Use AI-generated templates and content, then tailor them to fit each client's unique business and customer needs.
- **Stay Informed:** Keep up with the latest trends in CX and customer behavior to offer fresh, innovative strategies.
- **Data Interpretation:** Develop strong analytical skills to turn customer data into actionable insights.
- **Focus on Results:** Prioritize creating measurable improvements in customer satisfaction, retention, and loyalty.

As a CX consultant, AI can significantly enhance your ability to gather and interpret data. Still, the key to success lies in understanding your client's unique challenges and creating tailored human-centered solutions. CX consulting is not just about solving problems – anticipating customer needs, building trust, and delivering experiences that set businesses apart. Specializing in specific industries, staying connected with other CX professionals, and attending industry conferences will help you grow your expertise. Embrace continuous learning and networking to remain at the forefront of CX consulting and help your clients thrive.

75. Social Media Customer Support

Helping customers through social media requires crafting positive, meaningful interactions in real-time. If you thrive on connecting with people and solving problems with a personal touch, Social Media Customer Support might be the perfect side hustle for you. With AI tools like ChatGPT, you can speed up your workflow by generating response templates, creating proactive engagement strategies, and even developing crisis management plans. Combining your communication skills with AI will allow you to support customers efficiently, ensuring they feel valued and heard on their favorite platforms.

How to Use AI Tools:

- **Response Templates:** Use ChatGPT to draft quick, brand-consistent replies for common customer inquiries.
- **Engagement Strategies:** Generate ideas for posts that proactively engage customers and address potential concerns.
- **Escalation Flowcharts:** Create flowcharts to determine the best steps for handling complex customer issues.
- **Sentiment Analysis:** Develop frameworks to analyze customer sentiment based on social media mentions and feedback.

Potential Earnings:

- $14 - $35+ per hour, depending on your expertise and the scope of the social media accounts you're managing.

Platforms to Use:

- **Hootsuite** or **Sprout Social:** This is forThis is for managing multiple social media channels efficiently.
- **Zendesk:** This is for managing customer support tickets and tracking history.
- **Brand24:** This monitors brand mentions and analyzes social media sentiment.
- **Upwork** or **Fiverr:** This is for finding freelance clients and offering social media customer support services.

Quick-Start Steps:

1. **Learn the Platforms:** Understand how significant social media sites like Facebook, Twitter, and Instagram operate.
2. **Sharpen Communication Skills:** Develop clear, professional, and friendly responses that align with the brand's

voice.

3. **Build a Portfolio:** Create sample customer service responses and case studies for various scenarios.
4. **Find Opportunities:** Set up profiles on freelance platforms or apply directly to companies needing social media support.

Tips for Success:

- **Customize Responses:** Use AI-generated templates as a starting point but constantly tailor them to the brand and specific customer interaction.
- **Stay on Top of Trends:** Stay updated on the latest social media features and tools to remain effective.
- **Master Conflict Resolution:** Learn to handle difficult situations patiently, turning negative customer experiences into positive outcomes.
- **Proactive Approach:** Identify potential issues before they escalate by monitoring sentiment and addressing concerns early.

When working in social media customer support, you aim to blend speed with empathy, ensuring customers feel heard while keeping things efficient. AI tools are excellent for speeding up repetitive tasks, but your human touch will be what keeps the interactions personal and genuine. Specializing in specific industries, developing crisis management skills, and networking with other professionals can open the door to working with more prominent brands. Staying informed on social media algorithm updates and customer service best practices will help you thrive in this role.

76. Customer Feedback Analysis and Reporting

Understanding customers' feelings about a product or service is vital to success. If you're enthusiastic about helping companies improve through data-driven insights, Customer Feedback Analysis and Reporting might be your perfect side hustle. With AI tools like ChatGPT, you can accelerate the process by generating data visualization ideas, crafting detailed report templates, and developing actionable recommendation frameworks. By combining AI-generated resources with your analytical skills, you can turn raw feedback into valuable insights that businesses can act on to enhance their offerings.

How to Use AI Tools:

- **Survey Creation:** Use ChatGPT to generate survey question ideas and feedback collection methods.
- **Data Organization:** Create categorization and tagging systems for organizing qualitative feedback.
- **Report Templates:** Develop templates for executive summaries and detailed feedback reports.
- **Actionable Recommendations:** Generate ideas for recommendations based on customer feedback patterns.

Potential Earnings:

- $15 - $24+ per hour, depending on the scope and complexity of the analysis.

Platforms to Use:

- **SurveyMonkey** or **Typeform:** This is used to collect customer feedback efficiently.
- **Tableau** or **Sigma:** For creating data visualizations that make your insights clear.
- **NVivo** or **Atlas.ti:** To conduct in-depth qualitative data analysis.

Quick-Start Steps:

1. **Master Data Analysis:** Develop strong skills in analyzing and interpreting customer feedback.
2. **Learn Visualization Tools:** Familiarize yourself with data visualization platforms and qualitative analysis software.
3. **Create Sample Reports:** Use publicly available datasets for sample feedback analysis reports.
4. **Build a Portfolio:** Showcase your analytical skills and insights in a professional portfolio.

Tips for Success:

- **Leverage AI Smartly:** Use AI-generated insights as a starting point, but apply your critical thinking to create meaningful, actionable recommendations.
- **Simplify Complex Data:** Focus on translating complicated data sets into clear, practical advice for your clients.
- **Stay Industry-Savvy:** Keep up with industry trends and benchmarks to provide relevant context for your analysis.
- **Hone Presentation Skills:** Develop your ability to communicate your findings through reports and presentations effectively.

As a feedback analyst, AI will streamline data processing and highlight initial insights, but your ability to understand business contexts and provide strategic recommendations is critical. You can become an expert in your niche by specializing in particular industries or focusing on certain types of feedback. Ethical practices, solid analytical skills, and transparent reporting are crucial for success in this role. Stay ahead by continuously learning new tools and techniques, including predictive analytics, to distinguish your services in the market.

77. Online Community Management

Building and nurturing an engaged online community is a rewarding way to connect people, spark conversations, and create a space for shared interests. Online Community Management might be your perfect side hustle if you enjoy fostering meaningful interactions and guiding discussions. Using AI tools like ChatGPT, you can enhance your efforts with ideas for engagement content, automated moderation tools, and even strategies for growing the community. Pairing these AI-generated resources with your communication skills will allow you to create a thriving, supportive online environment.

How to Use AI Tools:

- **Engagement Content:** Use ChatGPT to generate ideas for discussion topics and posts that get people talking.
- **Welcome Messages:** Create automated welcome messages and FAQ responses to greet new members.
- **Moderation Guidelines:** Develop clear guidelines for managing conflicts and moderating posts.
- **Event Ideas:** Keep members engaged and generate ideas for community events, Q&A sessions, or special online gatherings.

Potential Earnings:

- $20 - $100+ per hour, depending on your experience and the size of the community you're managing.

Platforms to Use:

- **Facebook Groups** or **LinkedIn Groups:** For larger public or professional communities.
- **Discord** or **Slack:** Ideal for real-time community engagement and team-based interactions.
- **Reddit:** Great for managing niche communities and fostering topic-specific discussions.
- **Vanilla Forums** or **Discourse:** For hosted community platforms with customizable features.

Quick-Start Steps:

1. **Hone Your Communication Skills:** Develop strong communication and conflict resolution abilities.
2. **Learn Platform Features:** Familiarize yourself with community management tools on different platforms.
3. **Create a Sample Plan:** Draft a community management and engagement strategy to showcase your skills.
4. **Build a Portfolio:** Highlight community growth and engagement metrics from any relevant experience.

Tips for Success:

- **Personalize AI Content:** Use AI-generated ideas as a base, then adapt them to fit your community's culture and tone.
- **Foster Participation:** Encourage active involvement by creating a welcoming, inclusive environment for all members.
- **Stay Current:** Keep up with the latest platform features and online community trends to remain effective.
- **Handle Conflicts with Care:** Develop strategies for managing trolls, resolving disputes, and keeping conversations

positive.

AI tools can streamline community management tasks, like content creation and moderation. Still, a thriving community manager's real power lies in building solid connections and cultivating a sense of belonging. Your personal touch, insights, and ability to mediate are irreplaceable when creating a vibrant online space. Focus on ethical practices, networking within your niche, and staying up-to-date with the latest trends to maintain a healthy, engaged community and grow your career in community management.

78. Customer Service Training and Development

Training customer service teams can be incredibly rewarding – especially when you're passionate about helping others develop skills that lead to better customer experiences. Customer Service Training and Development could be your perfect opportunity if you love teaching and can connect with people. With AI tools like ChatGPT, you can elevate your training programs by generating interactive role-play scenarios, creating tailored course content, and developing engaging assessment materials. Pairing these AI-generated resources with your expertise allows you to deliver comprehensive, practical training programs that empower customer service teams to excel.

How to Use AI Tools:

- **Role-Play Scenarios:** Use ChatGPT to generate diverse customer interaction situations for practice during training.
- **Custom Training Modules:** Create personalized training content tailored to company needs and customer service standards.
- **Assessments:** Develop quizzes and evaluations to track learner progress and reinforce critical concepts.
- **Engagement Ideas:** Generate gamification elements like challenges or rewards to make the training interactive and fun.

Potential Earnings:

- $12 - $30+ per hour for live training sessions, or create an online course and charge $20+ per participant.

Platforms to Use:

- **Articulate 360** or **Adobe Captivate:** This is used to create professional e-learning courses.
- **Zoom** or **Microsoft Teams:** Perfect for delivering virtual training sessions.
- **Kahoot!** or **Quizizz:** To create engaging, interactive quizzes and assessments
- **Udemy:** Ideal for hosting and selling your customer service training courses.

Quick-Start Steps:

1. **Understand Best Practices:** Master customer service principles and effective training methods.
2. **Develop Sample Materials:** Create training modules and interactive exercises to showcase your approach.
3. **Build a Portfolio:** Highlight success stories from previous training programs to attract clients.
4. **Network for Opportunities:** Connect with HR departments and business owners who must train their teams.

Tips for Success:

- **Tailor AI Content:** Start with AI-generated materials, but customize them to fit the industry and culture of the companies you're working with.
- **Emphasize Interaction:** Focus on hands-on learning with scenario-based exercises to keep trainees engaged.
- **Stay Current:** Follow trends in customer service and training technologies to offer up-to-date insights.
- **Hone Presentation Skills:** Develop robust facilitation techniques for delivering impactful and engaging training sessions.

Utilizing AI tools for content creation and scenario-building can enhance your customer service training programs. Still, the heart of your success will lie in your ability to connect with trainees and tailor your approach to their needs. Specializing in specific industries or training methods, maintaining a robust ethical approach, and keeping training inclusive and relevant are essential. 'You'll establish yourself as a go-to trainer in this valuable and in-demand field by continually refining your expertise and staying ahead of customer service trends.

79. Multi-Lingual Customer Support

Offering customer support in multiple languages is connecting with people across cultures and ensuring they feel understood and valued. If you have a knack for languages and enjoy helping others, Multi-lingual Customer Support is a side hustle that allows you to blend those skills seamlessly. With AI tools like ChatGPT, you can speed up your workflow by generating translations, crafting language-specific response templates, and developing cultural etiquette guidelines. Merging your language skills with AI-generated insights enables you to offer seamless, culturally aware support to a global audience.

How to Use AI Tools:

- **Translations:** Use ChatGPT to create initial translations for common customer inquiries and responses in multiple languages.
- **Response Templates:** Develop language-specific templates for various customer service scenarios, ensuring quick and efficient replies.
- **Cultural Sensitivity Guides:** Generate guides highlighting business etiquette and regional differences, ensuring

your responses are culturally appropriate.

- **Localized Engagement:** Create ideas for customer engagement strategies that resonate with different cultures and language preferences.

Potential Earnings:

- $11 - $30+ per hour, depending on the languages you speak and your level of expertise.

Platforms to Use:

- Zendesk or Freshdesk: For managing multi-lingual customer service tickets.
- Unbabel: For AI-powered translation assistance to help with real-time support.
- Skype or Zoom: Ideal for international voice and video customer service.

Quick-Start Steps:

1. **Language Proficiency:** Assess and improve your fluency in the languages in which you wish to offer support.
2. **Cultural Awareness:** Learn the business etiquette and cultural norms of the regions you'll interact with.
3. **Portfolio:** Showcase your language abilities and customer service skills with real-world examples.
4. **Freelance Profiles:** Set up accounts on Upwork or directly apply to multi-lingual support roles.

Tips for Success:

- **Refine Translations:** Use AI for initial translations but constantly fine-tune them to ensure accuracy and cultural relevance.
- **Cultural Sensitivity:** Stay updated on idioms and regional expressions to communicate naturally and appropriately.
- **Master Communication:** Hone your verbal and written communication in each language, focusing on clarity and empathy.
- **Patience with Barriers:** Language barriers can be challenging – stay calm, patient, and ready to clarify.

Your strength as a multi-lingual support specialist comes from offering effective communication beyond words, embracing cultural nuances, and creating a supportive customer experience. While AI can assist with translations and cultural insights, your expertise ensures accuracy and builds genuine connections. Consider specializing in in-demand language pairs and industries and focus on providing exceptional service to build a reputation for culturally aware, high-quality support. Stay committed to improving your language skills, expanding your cultural knowledge, and networking with other professionals to succeed in this field.

80. Customer Service Software Implementation and Optimization

Helping businesses improve their customer service operations by implementing and optimizing the right software solutions can be a game-changer. If you have a knack for tech and problem-solving, Customer Service Software Implementation and Optimization might be your perfect side hustle. Combining your technical expertise with AI tools like ChatGPT, you can streamline the process by generating implementation plans, creating user guides, and optimizing workflows. You'll play a critical role in helping businesses transform how they handle customer inquiries, ensuring smoother processes and happier customers.

How to Use AI Tools:

- **Software Comparison:** Use ChatGPT to create comparison matrices for various customer service software options tailored to client needs.
- **Implementation Plans:** Generate detailed, customized implementation timelines to help businesses onboard new systems smoothly.
- **User Guides:** Develop comprehensive manuals and training materials for employees learning to use the new software.
- **Workflow Optimization:** Create strategies for automating customer service processes and enhancing efficiency using AI insights.

Potential Earnings:

- $25 - $75+ per hour, depending on the scope and complexity of the project.

Platforms to Use:

- Salesforce Service Cloud: For CRM-based customer service solutions.
- Zendesk or Freshdesk: Popular helpdesk software for managing customer support tickets.
- Intercom: Ideal for conversational customer support through chat and messaging.

Quick-Start Steps:

1. **Master the Platforms:** Develop a deep understanding of popular customer service software solutions and how they can be optimized for various industries.
2. **Project Management Skills:** Build proficiency in managing projects, timelines, and change management during software rollouts.

3. **Create Case Studies:** Showcase hypothetical or past examples of successful implementations and optimizations.
4. **Network:** Connect with business owners, IT departments, and software vendors to find opportunities and build relationships.

Tips for Success:

- **Customize Solutions:** Use AI-generated content as a baseline but constantly tailor solutions to the specific needs of each business and their industry.
- **Stay Tech-Savvy:** Keep updated on the latest customer service technologies, software updates, and trends.
- **Measure ROI:** Develop strong analytical skills to track and communicate the return on investment for your clients.
- **Focus on Usability:** Prioritize user-friendly solutions that enhance customer service agents' productivity and overall customer satisfaction.

When working in customer service software consulting, you will combine technical knowledge with strategic thinking. AI can support you in generating ideas and streamlining processes. Still, your expertise in understanding client needs, integrating the right software, and ensuring the solutions are easy to use will set you apart. Specializing in specific tools or industries, maintaining client transparency, and continuously learning about new technologies will help you thrive in this dynamic and rewarding field. You'll create solutions that improve customer service by blending technology with human understanding.

81. Voice-Based Customer Service

Voice-based customer service involves assisting in phone interactions, voice-activated assistants, or smart speaker applications. This could be a great side hustle if you enjoy conversing with people and resolving their issues in real-time. With the help of AI tools like ChatGPT, you can streamline your service by generating conversational scripts, designing decision trees for voice response systems, and crafting intuitive voice user interfaces (VUIs). By merging your communication skills with AI-generated resources, you can offer seamless and efficient voice-based customer support that feels natural and personalized.

How to Use AI Tools:

- **Voice Scripts:** Use ChatGPT to create smooth, conversational voice scripts for customer scenarios.
- **Decision Trees:** Build interactive voice response (IVR) systems with decision trees that guide customers through their options.
- **Personalized Responses:** Develop personalized voice responses that adapt to customer history and preferences.
- **Voice Engagement:** Generate ideas for engaging customers through voice-based platforms, enhancing their overall experience.

Potential Earnings:

- $19 - $23+ per hour for voice support roles, or $20 - $40+ per hour for voice interface design projects.

Platforms to Use:

- **Amazon Connect:** For cloud-based voice customer service solutions.
- **Dialogflow:** For building conversational AI interfaces.
- **Twilio:** For creating programmable voice applications.

Quick-Start Steps:

1. **Refine Communication:** Develop strong verbal communication and active listening abilities.
2. **Learn the Tech:** Familiarize yourself with VUI design and voice technology tools.
3. **Create Samples:** Build example voice scripts and IVR systems for various sectors.
4. **Showcase Your Work:** Develop a portfolio highlighting your voice-based customer service skills.

Tips for Success:

- **Personalize the Script:** Start with AI-generated scripts, but ensure they feel conversational and empathetic.
- **Design with Intuition:** Create voice interfaces that are easy for customers to navigate, minimizing frustration.
- **Stay Current:** Keep up with advancements in voice recognition and AI-powered natural language processing.
- **Handle Difficult Calls:** Cultivate the ability to manage challenging conversations and resolve conflicts over the phone.

While AI can assist in scripting and designing efficient systems, the heart of voice-based customer service lies in the human connection. You'll offer the empathy and flexibility that customers need in real-time. Use AI as a tool to enhance your work, but never underestimate the power of your ability to listen, problem-solve, and respond to unique situations. Specializing in industries like healthcare, finance, or retail will allow you to grow your skills and reputation while staying up-to-date with emerging voice technologies and customer service trends, which will help you thrive in this dynamic field.

Miscellaneous Side Hustles

"Success usually comes to those who are too busy to be looking for it."
Henry David Thoreau

In this section, you'll discover a variety of unique and exciting side hustles that fall outside traditional categories, from virtual assistance to product testing. These opportunities allow you to leverage your skills, creativity, and AI tools like ChatGPT to enhance productivity, streamline tasks, and offer personalized services. Whether organizing someone's home, providing virtual support, or crafting tailored travel itineraries, each side hustle offers flexibility and the chance to impact your client's lives. Dive into these miscellaneous side hustles to find your perfect match!

82. Virtual Assistance

Virtual assistance offers an incredible opportunity to work remotely while supporting businesses and entrepreneurs. If you thrive on organization, communication, and efficiency, this side hustle might be a perfect fit for you. With AI tools like ChatGPT, you can elevate your virtual assistance services by automating routine tasks, brainstorming content, and managing communications. By combining your natural multitasking abilities with AI-generated insights, you can offer clients top-notch support that helps them focus on what really matters in their business.

How to Use AI Tools:

- **Draft Emails:** Use ChatGPT to quickly create professional email responses and client communications.
- **Content Ideas:** Generate ideas for social media posts, blog articles, or marketing campaigns.
- **Document Templates:** Create reports, presentations, or other recurring document templates.
- **FAQ Responses:** Develop automated replies for common client questions to save time.

Potential Earnings:

- $10 - $20+ per hour, depending on the scope of work and your level of expertise.

Platforms to Use:

- Upwork or Fiverr**:** To find virtual assistant job opportunities.

- Trello or Asana: For managing tasks and staying organized.
- Slack or Microsoft Teams: For seamless communication with clients.

Quick-Start Steps:

1. **Assess Your Skills:** Identify your strengths and the services you can offer effectively.
2. **Set Up Workspace:** Establish a home office with reliable tools, software, and internet.
3. **Create a Portfolio:** Showcase your skills, previous work, and any certifications you have.
4. **Find Clients:** Use freelance platforms or your network to find potential clients.

Tips for Success:

- **Refine with AI:** Start with AI-generated content, but tailor it to each client's unique needs and voice.
- **Master Time Management:** Develop strong prioritization and organization skills to handle multiple clients.
- **Stay Updated:** Keep learning about productivity tools, software, and relevant trends for your client's industry.
- **Communicate Effectively:** Proactively solve problems and ensure clear, professional communication.

Virtual assistance centers on building relationships and establishing trust. AI tools can make your job easier and more efficient, but remember, your real value comes from understanding your client's needs and delivering personalized, reliable support. Consider specializing in areas like project management, marketing, or customer service to differentiate yourself and increase your earning potential. Staying updated on new technology and productivity strategies will allow you to continue offering cutting-edge solutions to your clients, helping their businesses run smoothly while you thrive in this flexible side hustle path.

83. Legal Consulting

Do you have experience with legal matters and a passion for providing clear, actionable advice to clients? Legal consulting could be the perfect avenue for you to use your expertise and make a meaningful impact. With AI tools like ChatGPT, you can streamline your services by generating legal research summaries, drafting essential legal documents, and creating educational materials for clients. This powerful combination of AI assistance and your legal knowledge allows you to offer accessible and valuable legal guidance in a variety of areas.

How to Use AI Tools:

- **Legal Summaries:** Use ChatGPT to generate concise summaries of legal cases, statutes, or regulations.
- **Document Templates:** Create templates for common legal documents like contracts, NDAs, or wills.
- **Client Education:** Develop FAQ sheets or guides on key legal topics to help educate clients.

- **Legal Strategy Outlines:** Generate detailed outlines for legal strategies and proposals based on client needs.

Potential Earnings:

- $30 - $100+ per hour, depending on the complexity of the legal matters and your level of expertise.

Platforms to Use:

- **LegalZoom** or **Rocket Lawyer:** For document templates and legal resource materials.
- **Clio:** To manage your legal practice efficiently.
- **LinkedIn:** To network with professionals and attract potential clients.
- **Upwork:** For freelance legal consulting opportunities.

Quick-Start Steps:

1. **Ensure Qualifications:** Make sure you have the required legal certifications and licenses.
2. **Identify Expertise:** Clarify your areas of legal specialization and target clientele.
3. **Create a Portfolio:** Develop a collection of sample legal documents and consulting work to showcase your expertise.
4. **Establish Your Online Presence:** Build a professional website or LinkedIn profile to market your consulting services.

Tips for Success:

- **Refine with Expertise:** Start with AI-generated content, but apply your knowledge to ensure it meets the highest legal standards.
- **Stay Informed:** Continuously update your understanding of laws, regulations, and industry trends relevant to your practice.
- **Simplify Complex Concepts:** Develop strong communication skills to translate complex legal jargon into clear, actionable advice.
- **Deliver Practical Solutions:** Focus on providing clients with realistic, actionable strategies they can easily implement.

AI can improve efficiency as a legal consultant, but the real value lies in your deep legal insight and judgment. You can create lasting client relationships built on trust by ensuring confidentiality, maintaining ethical standards, and applying your specialized expertise. Consider focusing on areas like intellectual property, small business law, or estate planning to differentiate yourself. Additionally, networking with other legal professionals and staying updated on the latest developments in law and legal tech can enhance your consulting services. You'll confidently help clients navigate their legal challenges by offering clear, practical legal guidance.

84. Travel Planning

Do you love crafting unforgettable travel experiences and helping others explore the world? Travel planning might be the perfect way to combine your passion for adventure with a rewarding side hustle. Using AI tools like ChatGPT, you can elevate your services, generate itinerary ideas, design personalized travel guides, and develop budget-friendly options tailored to your clients' preferences. Combining your travel expertise with AI allows you to provide well-organized, unique travel experiences that your clients will rave about.

How to Use AI Tools:

- **Itinerary Ideas:** Use ChatGPT to create unique, detailed travel itineraries based on client interests and destination preferences.
- **Personalized Guides:** Craft customized travel guides filled with local attractions, hidden gems, and insider tips.
- **Budget-Friendly Plans:** Develop budget breakdowns and strategies to help clients maximize their travel expenses.
- **Packing Lists:** Generate packing lists tailored to each client's destination, season, and travel style.

Potential Earnings:

- $30 - $100+ per hour, depending on the complexity of the trip and your expertise.

Platforms to Use:

- TripAdvisor: For researching destinations and gathering reviews.
- Booking.com or Expedia: To book accommodations and flights.
- Instagram or Pinterest: To gather and share visual inspiration for travel itineraries.
- Upwork: For finding freelance travel planning opportunities.

Quick-Start Steps:

1. **Build Destination Knowledge:** Familiarize yourself with various destinations, local customs, and travel logistics.
2. **Create Sample Itineraries:** Develop itineraries that cater to different types of travelers and budgets.
3. **Establish Your Online Presence:** Set up a website or social media profile to showcase your services and expertise.
4. **Network:** Build connections with travel suppliers, local guides, and potential clients to enhance your offerings.

Tips for Success:

- **Customize with Personal Insights:** Start with AI-generated ideas, but use your firsthand knowledge to create unique, tailored experiences for each client.
- **Stay Informed:** Stay current on travel trends, visa requirements, and health advisories to provide accurate and up-to-date advice.
- **Develop Industry Relationships:** Form partnerships with hotels, tour operators, and local businesses to offer exclusive deals and insider access.
- **Focus on the Experience:** Craft travel plans beyond typical tourist traps, offering your clients memorable, personalized experiences.

Your attention to detail and understanding of destinations are key to creating seamless and enjoyable journeys in travel planning. AI can assist with logistics and ideas, but your personal insights and dedication to crafting unique travel experiences make all the difference. By specializing in specific destinations or types of travel, networking with industry professionals, and staying updated on travel technology and trends, you can build a successful travel planning business that keeps clients coming back for more.

85. Event Planning

There's something gratifying about orchestrating an event that flows seamlessly from start to finish. Whether it's a wedding, a corporate function, or a community fundraiser, being the mastermind behind a successful gathering requires creativity, meticulous planning, and top-notch coordination. With AI tools like ChatGPT, you can streamline your event planning process, from brainstorming unique themes to crafting detailed timelines and managing complex budgets. Combining these AI resources with your personal expertise allows you to create smooth, unforgettable events that exceed your client's expectations.

How to Use AI Tools:

- **Event Themes**: Use ChatGPT to generate fresh, unique event themes and concepts.
- **Timelines**: Create detailed event timelines and day-of checklists.
- **Budget Plans**: Develop budget templates and cost estimation guides.
- **Vendor Coordination**: Generate vendor questionnaires and comparison matrices.

Potential Earnings:

- $30 - $125+ per hour, or $300 - $5,000+ per event, depending on the scope and complexity.

Platforms to Use:

- **Eventbrite:** For ticket sales and event promotion.
- **Prism:** For virtual venue layouts and seating arrangements.
- **Slack** or **Asana:** For team coordination and task management.
- **Upwork:** To find event planning clients.

Quick-Start Steps:

1. **Build Organizational Skills**: Strengthen your ability to manage complex details and timelines.
2. **Develop a Portfolio**: Create sample event plans and mood boards to showcase your creativity.
3. **Network with Vendors**: Establish connections with reliable vendors and service providers.
4. **Establish an Online Presence**: Set up a professional website or social media pages to market your services.

Tips for Success:

- **Use AI for Inspiration**: Leverage AI-generated ideas but tailor them to suit each client's preferences and logistics.
- **Stay Current on Trends**: Keep updated on the latest event trends, venue options, and local regulations.
- **Prepare Contingency Plans**: Always have backup plans for potential challenges like weather or vendor cancellations.
- **Focus on Personalization**: Craft unique, personalized experiences that align with the client's vision and budget.

Event planning combines creativity, organization, and problem-solving into a seamless process. AI helps boost efficiency and creativity, and your expertise ensures every detail aligns perfectly. Specializing in particular event types, from corporate events to weddings, and staying informed about the latest event technologies, will allow you to stand out in this dynamic field. Building strong vendor relationships and offering unique, memorable experiences will ensure your clients keep coming back for more.

86. Marriage Officiant

Few things are as meaningful as helping two people celebrate the start of their life together. As a marriage officiant, you can guide couples through one of the most important moments of their lives. Whether it's a traditional ceremony or something uniquely personalized, your role is to create a memorable and heartfelt experience. By using AI tools like ChatGPT, you can elevate your services – creating customized vows, drafting ceremony scripts, and ensuring the day flows seamlessly.

How to Use AI Tools:

- **Ceremony Scripts**: Use ChatGPT to craft personalized ceremony scripts that reflect the couple's values and relationship.

- **Vows**: Develop vow templates that couples can customize to express their unique love stories.
- **Speech Writing**: Generate ideas for opening remarks, blessings, or closing statements.
- **Ceremony Timeline**: Create detailed timelines for the ceremony, ensuring smooth transitions between different elements.

Potential Earnings:

- $300 - $500+ per ceremony, depending on your level of involvement, customization, and travel.

Platforms to Use:

- **The Knot** or **WeddingWire**: Market your services to couples planning their weddings.
- **Thumbtack:** Find local couples searching for officiants.
- **Upwork:** Offer custom ceremony script writing or vow creation services.
- **Instagram:** Showcase your officiating style with testimonials, ceremony snippets, and client reviews.

Quick-Start Steps:

1. **Get Ordained**: Complete the necessary steps to become legally ordained (many services are available online).
2. **Build a Portfolio**: Create sample ceremony scripts and collect testimonials from previous weddings.
3. **Learn Local Requirements**: Ensure you're familiar with the legal paperwork required to officiate weddings in your area.
4. **Market Yourself**: Develop a professional website or use social media to attract engaged couples.

Tips for Success:

- **Personalize Every Ceremony**: Use AI-generated content as a foundation, but always customize it to reflect the couple's story and preferences.
- **Polish Your Public Speaking**: Practice delivering ceremonies with clarity, emotion, and confidence.
- **Network with Venues**: Build relationships with local wedding venues to become a recommended officiant.
- **Adapt to Changes**: Be flexible and ready to accommodate any last-minute adjustments, whether due to weather, timing, or personal requests.

Becoming a marriage officiant is not just about leading a ceremony – it's about creating an unforgettable experience that celebrates love. AI can help streamline script writing and planning. Still, your personal touch and connection with the couple make each ceremony spa. Focusing on the couple's needs, staying current with ceremony trends, and continually refining your public speaking and presentation skills will help build your reputation and ensure success as an officiant.

87. Pet Sitting

Caring for someone's pet while they're away is a unique and rewarding responsibility. It's not just about providing food and exercise – it's about ensuring the animal feels comfortable, safe, and loved in your care. If you're passionate about animals and want to offer top-tier pet sitting services, AI tools like ChatGPT can help you by generating personalized care schedules, pet profiles, and communication templates for keeping pet owners informed. Combining your dedication to pets with AI assistance can provide a seamless and enjoyable experience for both pets and their owners.

How to Use AI Tools:

- **Care Schedules**: Use ChatGPT to create customized care routines, including feeding times, walks, and medication reminders.
- **Pet Profiles**: Generate personalized profiles with detailed information such as dietary restrictions, favorite toys, and temperament.
- **Owner Updates**: Develop communication templates for sending daily updates, photos, and notes on the pet's well-being.
- **FAQs**: Create an FAQ sheet to help potential clients understand your services, rates, and policies.

Potential Earnings:

- $15 - $25+ per hour, depending on your experience and the level of care required.

Platforms to Use:

- Rover or Wag!: Find pet sitting opportunities in your local area.
- PetBacker: Build and grow your pet care business with easy booking management.
- Instagram or Facebook: Promote your services, showcase happy pets, and attract new clients.

Quick-Start Steps:

1. **Get Experience**: Familiarize yourself with various pet behaviors and care needs by volunteering or taking on small jobs.
2. **Create a Profile**: Highlight your pet care expertise, any relevant certifications, and your love for animals.

3. **Organize Your Services**: Develop a system for managing bookings, updating pet owners, and tracking care schedules.

4. **Build Your Reputation**: Start gathering reviews and testimonials from happy clients to build trust and attract more business.

Tips for Success:

- **Customize Your Approach**: Use AI-generated care plans as a baseline, but adapt them to each pet's unique preferences.
- **Communicate Effectively**: Keep pet owners updated with detailed information about their pet's day.
- **Keep Learning**: Stay informed about pet care, first aid, and behavioral trends to offer the best service possible.
- **Create Comfort**: Focus on making pets feel secure and at ease while under your care.

Pet sitting is about building trust and creating a nurturing environment for pets, ensuring their owners feel confident while away. AI can help you streamline your processes, but your attention and love for animals will set you apart. Consider offering additional services like dog walking or pet grooming to grow your business, and always be looking for ways to expand your knowledge and expertise in pet care.

88. House Sitting

House sitting is more than just watching over someone's home – it's about providing peace of mind to homeowners while they're away. Whether it's making sure plants stay hydrated, collecting the mail, or keeping an eye on the property's security, your attention to detail and reliability make all the difference. With AI tools like ChatGPT, you can take your house sitting services to the next level by creating home care checklists, developing status reports, and staying in constant communication with homeowners. Combining your dedication with AI-enhanced tools, you can ensure each home is cared for exactly as the homeowner expects.

How to Use AI Tools:

- **House Care Checklists**: Use ChatGPT to create customized checklists for tasks like plant care, mail collection, and property checks.
- **Homeowner Updates**: Generate templates for daily or weekly status reports to keep homeowners informed while they're away.
- **Security Routines**: Develop personalized home security routines, from locking windows to setting alarms.
- **Service FAQs**: Create a list of frequently asked questions to outline your services and policies for potential clients.

Potential Earnings:

- $30 - $80+ per day, or $500 to $2,500+ per month, depending on responsibilities, location, and the length of the stay.

Platforms to Use:

- TrustedHousesitters: A platform for finding international house sitting opportunities.
- MindMyHouse: Connect with homeowners looking for responsible house sitters.
- Nextdoor: Find local house sitting gigs by networking with neighbors.

Quick-Start Steps:

1. **Build a Profile**: Highlight your reliability, house sitting or pet care experience, and relevant skills.
2. **Get References**: Secure references from previous homeowners or employers to build trust.
3. **List Services Clearly**: Detail the specific services you offer and your availability.
4. **Background Check**: Consider getting a background check to boost your credibility.

Tips for Success:

- **Customize Checklists**: Use AI-generated checklists as a base, but tailor them to meet each home's specific needs.
- **Communicate Regularly**: Keep homeowners updated with photos and notes, giving them peace of mind.
- **Stay Organized**: Keep detailed records of tasks, schedules, and any issues that arise.
- **Prepare for the Unexpected**: Be ready to handle minor repairs or unexpected situations like a pet emergency.

Being a house sitter is about trust, responsibility, and providing a worry-free experience for homeowners. AI can help streamline communication, organization, attention to detail, and personal touch that homeowners will appreciate most. Focus on being proactive, reliable, and adaptable, and consider offering additional services like pet care or minor maintenance to set yourself apart. Staying connected with your clients and going the extra mile will help you build a strong reputation, leading to repeat business and referrals.

89. Voiceover Work

Lending your voice to bring stories, characters, and brands to life is an enriching experience. Voiceover work allows you to express creativity in ways that reach audiences worldwide, whether through commercials, audiobooks, or animation. By pairing your vocal talent with AI tools like ChatGPT, you can amplify your services – using it to generate script ideas, craft character profiles, and even improve voice modulation. Combining these AI-generated resources with your skills will help you deliver captivating and professional performances that leave a lasting impression.

How to Use AI Tools:

- **Script Variations**: Use ChatGPT to generate script variations for different tones, moods, and styles.
- **Character Profiles**: Create detailed character backstories to help you embody roles with more depth and personality.
- **Vocal Exercises**: Develop vocal warm-up exercises to ensure consistent performance quality.
- **Demo Reel Ideas**: Generate ideas for demo reels to showcase your versatility and range.

Potential Earnings:

- $100 - $500+ per hour for professional gigs or $50 - $250+ per finished hour for audiobooks.

Platforms to Use:

- **Voices:** For finding voiceover jobs across various industries.
- **ACX (Audiobook Creation Exchange):** For audiobook narration opportunities.
- **Fiverr** or **Upwork:** For freelance voiceover gigs and quick projects.

Quick-Start Steps:

1. **Invest in Equipment**: Get a quality microphone, audio interface, and recording software to produce professional sound.
2. **Create a Demo Reel**: Showcase your vocal range and styles through a polished demo reel.
3. **Set Up a Recording Space**: Ensure you have proper acoustics and soundproofing for high-quality recordings.
4. **Join Marketplaces**: Build profiles on voiceover platforms and start auditioning for gigs.

Tips for Success:

- **Adapt AI Content**: Use AI-generated ideas as a foundation, but let your unique voice and style shine through.
- **Expand Your Range**: Practice different voices, accents, and styles to boost versatility and opportunities.
- **Consistent Practice**: Improve vocal control, stamina, and tone with regular voice training.
- **Stay Informed**: Keep up with industry trends, new platforms, and voiceover technologies to stay competitive.

Being a voiceover artist requires more than a great voice – it's about delivering emotion, clarity, and character that captivates listeners. AI can support script ideas and practice, but your voice and performance truly make the magic happen. Focus on building your niche, whether it's commercials, narration, or animation, and always be professional and reliable. Networking with content creators and audio professionals and refining your craft will help you grow a successful voiceover side hustle.

90. Transcription Services

Transforming spoken words into precise, readable text is a skill that's more valuable than ever, especially in today's fast-paced, content-driven world. As a transcriptionist, you become the bridge between audio and text, creating accessible records of interviews, podcasts, lectures, and even specialized fields like medical and legal content. With AI tools like speech recognition software and ChatGPT, you can take your transcription services to the next level – speeding up initial drafts, organizing content, and ensuring that industry-specific terminology is spot on. Combined with your sharp listening skills and meticulous attention to detail, this side hustle can become a thriving business.

How to Use AI Tools:

- **Automated Transcripts**: Use speech recognition software to create rough drafts of transcripts, cutting down initial typing time.
- **Industry Glossaries**: Leverage ChatGPT to generate lists of relevant terminology for specific fields, such as law, medicine, or academia.
- **Format Templates**: To streamline your process, create templates for different transcription styles, such as verbatim or clean read.
- **Editing Macros**: Develop macros for repetitive tasks like common edits or formatting adjustments.

Potential Earnings:

- $17 - $25+ per hour for general transcription, or significantly more in specialized fields like legal or medical transcription.

Platforms to Use:

- **Rev** or **TranscribeMe:** This is used to find transcription jobs across various industries.
- **Otter.ai** or **Trint:** For AI-assisted transcription to accelerate your workflow.
- **Upwork** or **Fiverr:** This is for freelance transcription gigs and building your client base.

Quick-Start Steps:

1. **Improve Typing Speed**: Practice to increase your typing speed and accuracy, as this directly impacts your productivity.
2. **Diversify Your Audio Samples**: Work with different accents and audio qualities to hone your listening and

transcription accuracy.

3. **Join Platforms**: Set up profiles on transcription platforms or freelance marketplaces to find gigs.

4. **Specialize**: To boost your earning potential, consider focusing on a particular niche, such as medical or legal transcription.

Tips for Success:

- **Refine AI Drafts**: Use AI-generated transcripts as a base, but ensure accuracy and readability by refining the text yourself.

- **Adapt to Accents**: Train your ear to understand a variety of accents, speaking speeds, and background noise levels.

- **Stay Current**: Keep up-to-date with industry-specific terminology and formatting or style requirements changes.

- **Balance Accuracy and Speed**: Work on improving both speed and accuracy, as they are key to success in transcription.

Your attention to detail, ability to capture nuances, and precision in delivering a polished final product set you apart in transcription. AI can help you work faster, but your role in refining, editing, and ensuring the accuracy of the final transcript is indispensable. Maintain confidentiality, follow ethical guidelines, and consistently meet deadlines. Building a strong reputation for reliability and quality work will lead to more opportunities. Diversifying into proofreading, closed captioning, or specialized transcription can further elevate your business.

91. Translation Services

Bringing the essence of one language into another is no small feat – it requires not just fluency but an in-depth understanding of cultural nuances, idiomatic expressions, and context. Translation services might be your perfect path if you're passionate about bridging linguistic gaps and helping people communicate across cultures. Combining your language expertise with AI tools like machine translation software and ChatGPT can streamline the translation process – automating first drafts, creating glossaries for technical terms, and ensuring consistency across large projects. These tools, paired with your nuanced understanding of language and culture, enable you to deliver high-quality translations that resonate in meaning and tone.

How to Use AI Tools:

- **Initial Drafts**: Use machine translation tools to generate the first draft of your translations, saving time on repetitive tasks.

- **Terminology Lists**: Leverage ChatGPT to build industry-specific glossaries, ensuring accurate and consistent use of terms across projects.

- **Templates**: Create translation templates for different types of documents, such as legal contracts, marketing copy, or technical manuals.

- **Consistency Checks**: Develop automated checks for maintaining consistency in terminology and phrasing throughout large, complex projects.

Potential Earnings:

- $15 - $25+ per hour, with higher rates for rare language pairs, specialized fields, or highly technical content.

Platforms to Use:

- **ProZ:** A robust platform for translation jobs and networking with fellow translators.
- **TranslatorsCafe:** Offers a variety of translation opportunities across multiple industries.
- **Gengo** or **Translate.com:** Ideal for picking up online translation work and building experience.
- **Upwork:** This is for freelancers seeking broader translation and language services opportunities.

Quick-Start Steps:

1. **Assess Language Proficiency**: Ensure your fluency is at a professional level and consider certifications if necessary.
2. **Familiarize with Tools**: Get comfortable using CAT tools and translation software to streamline your workflow.
3. **Create Profiles**: Showcase your language pairs and specializations on translation platforms.
4. **Build a Portfolio**: Start by translating public domain texts or offering pro bono work to build a solid portfolio.

Tips for Success:

- **Refine AI Drafts**: Use AI-generated translations as a foundation, but always refine for accuracy, natural flow, and cultural relevance.
- **Keep Languages Current**: Stay updated on both languages you work with, including modern slang and cultural references.
- **Specialize**: Develop legal, medical, or technical translation expertise to command higher rates.
- **Cultural Sensitivity**: Ensure your translations are accurate and culturally appropriate for the target audience.

Translation services require more than just converting words from one language to another – they demand a deep understanding of cultural contexts and linguistic subtleties. AI tools can enhance your efficiency, but your language mastery and cultural sensitivity will set you apart. Ethical considerations, such as maintaining confidentiality and ensuring the integrity of the original message, are essential. Building expertise in specific fields and developing localization skills can help expand your scope. Continuously honing your language abilities and networking with other translators will open doors to more opportunities in this rewarding field.

92. Data Entry

Accuracy, speed, and attention to detail – if you pride yourself on these qualities, data entry might be your ideal side hustle. Whether you're inputting numbers, names, or inventory details, data entry plays a crucial role in keeping businesses organized and efficient. By incorporating AI tools like optical character recognition (OCR) software and ChatGPT, you can take your data entry services to the next level – automating some of the more tedious tasks while focusing on what matters most: precision. Combining your sharp typing skills with AI-driven efficiency makes you a powerhouse of productivity, capable of efficiently handling large volumes of data.

How to Use AI Tools:

- **OCR Software**: Use optical character recognition tools to digitize printed or handwritten documents for faster entry.
- **Data Systems**: Leverage ChatGPT to develop data categorization systems, making the organization of large datasets more manageable.
- **Templates & Macros**: Create automated templates and macros for repetitive tasks to save time.
- **Data Cleaning**: Develop scripts to clean and validate data, ensuring accuracy across the board.

Potential Earnings:

- $10 - $20+ per hour, depending on the complexity of the data and your speed.

Platforms to Use:

- **Clickworker:** For micro-tasks, including data entry and categorization.
- **Amazon Mechanical Turk:** Ideal for a wide variety of data entry projects.
- **Upwork** or **Fiverr:** For freelance data entry gigs and building long-term client relationships.

Quick-Start Steps:

1. **Typing Skills**: Hone your speed and accuracy through practice and online typing tests.
2. **Software Familiarity**: Learn to use common data entry programs and spreadsheet tools like Excel or Google Sheets.
3. **Create Profiles**: Set up accounts on platforms like Upwork or Clickworker, highlighting your data entry expertise.
4. **Certifications**: Consider certifications in data management or relevant software to boost your credibility.

Tips for Success:

- **AI-Assisted Accuracy**: Use AI tools for initial data capture but always verify for quality and completeness.
- **Maintain Speed & Precision**: Develop methods to increase your typing speed while minimizing errors.
- **Stay Updated**: Keep up with data privacy laws and best practices to ensure you handle information ethically.
- **Build a Reputation**: Deliver consistent, high-quality work to earn trust and build a loyal client base.

Data entry may seem straightforward, but maintaining accuracy across large datasets is no small feat. AI tools can help streamline and speed up the process, but you are responsible for ensuring data integrity. Ethical considerations, such as protecting sensitive information and adhering to privacy regulations, are paramount. By specializing in specific fields like medical or financial data, continually improving your typing speed, and staying updated on the latest technologies, you can build a strong foundation for a sustainable and profitable data entry side hustle.

93. Survey Participation

Have you ever wanted to share your opinion and get paid for it? Survey participation gives you the chance to do just that! Whether you're offering feedback on products, services, or market trends, your insights are valuable to companies looking to improve. With AI tools like ChatGPT, you can maximize your survey-taking efficiency by generating thoughtful responses, organizing your schedule, and ensuring you never miss a high-paying opportunity. Combining your personal experiences with AI-enhanced responses can help you provide valuable insights while optimizing your time.

How to Use AI Tools:

- **Open-Ended Responses**: Use ChatGPT to brainstorm ideas for more detailed, engaging answers to open-ended questions.
- **Survey Schedules**: Generate reminders and schedules for high-paying or time-sensitive survey opportunities.
- **Response Templates**: Create templates for frequently asked survey questions to improve efficiency.
- **Tracking System**: Develop a system for tracking your survey completions and earnings over time.

Potential Earnings:

- $1 - $20+ per survey, or $50 - $250+ per hour for focus groups or in-depth studies.

Platforms to Use:

- **Swagbucks** or **Survey Junkie:** For a variety of online surveys and rewards.
- **Respondent.io:** High-paying research studies and focus groups.
- **Amazon Mechanical Turk:** Micro-tasks including surveys for quick, smaller earnings.

Quick-Start Steps:

1. **Multiple Profiles**: Set up accounts on various survey platforms to increase opportunities.
2. **Detailed Demographics**: Fill out your profile with detailed demographic information for better survey matches.
3. **Separate Email**: Create a dedicated email address for all your survey-related notifications.
4. **Start Small**: Begin with shorter surveys to build your profile and increase eligibility for higher-paying options.

Tips for Success:

- **Be Honest**: Use AI-generated ideas to enhance your responses, but always provide genuine feedback.
- **Targeted Surveys**: Focus on surveys that align with your interests or expertise for higher completion rates.
- **Consistency**: Ensure your responses are consistent and clear to maintain credibility across platforms.
- **Track Your Progress**: Monitor your time spent on surveys and earnings to evaluate the worth of your efforts.

AI can help streamline your survey participation, but your authenticity and thoughtful input are key to success in this side hustle. Ethical practices, such as providing honest feedback and respecting survey confidentiality, ensure the integrity of your responses. Consider specializing in surveys that align with your knowledge or interests to maximize your earnings. With a little effort and organization, survey participation can become a fun and rewarding way to supplement your income, all from the comfort of your home!

94. Product Testing

Do you love trying out new products before they hit the market? Product testing could be the perfect side hustle for you! As a product tester, you'll get your hands on a variety of items, from tech gadgets to beauty products, all while helping companies improve their offerings. With AI tools like ChatGPT, you can take your testing to the next level by creating detailed review templates, organizing comparison lists, and structuring your feedback reports. Combining your observational skills with AI resources will allow you to deliver high-quality, insightful product reviews that companies can really use.

How to Use AI Tools:

- **Product Testing Checklists**: Use ChatGPT to generate detailed checklists for evaluating various product features.
- **Review Templates**: Create templates for writing consistent, thorough reviews across different product categories.
- **Pros and Cons Lists**: Develop structured formats to highlight the strengths and weaknesses of each product.
- **Testing Scenarios**: Generate creative ideas for unique use cases and real-world testing situations.

Potential Earnings:

- According to ZipRecruiter, you could earn $14 - $57+ per hour.

Platforms to Use:

- **UserTesting:** For testing digital products and websites.
- **PineCone Research:** For consumer product testing.
- **BetaBound:** For beta testing tech products.
- **ZipRecruiter:** For finding product testing gigs.

Quick-Start Steps:

1. **Sign Up**: Join multiple product testing platforms and fill out your profile in detail to get more opportunities.
2. **Hone Your Skills**: Practice being observant and analytical when testing products.
3. **Stay Organized**: Develop a system for recording and documenting your test results.
4. **Build Visibility**: Consider starting a blog, YouTube channel, or social media presence to showcase your product reviews.

Tips for Success:

- **Personalized Observations**: Use AI-generated templates for structure, but always include your honest and unique insights.
- **Balanced Feedback**: Provide a well-rounded review by highlighting the product's strengths and areas for improvement.
- **Thorough Testing**: Ensure you test the product in various scenarios to give comprehensive feedback.
- **Actionable Input**: Offer constructive criticism that companies can use to refine their products before release.

Though AI can streamline your workflow, your personal experiences and honest, thorough feedback are what really set you apart in the world of product testing. Companies rely on testers to provide genuine, insightful reviews that help them fine-tune their offerings. By specializing in certain product categories and continuously building your expertise, you can establish yourself as a trusted product tester, opening doors to more exclusive and higher-paying testing opportunities. Always stay honest, respect confidentiality agreements, and aim to make your feedback as valuable as possible to keep growing in this exciting field.

95. Mystery Shopping

Have you ever wanted to blend into the crowd while secretly assessing the service and experience at your favorite stores or restaurants? That's the fun and intrigue of mystery shopping! As a mystery shopper, you get to act as a regular customer while evaluating everything from customer service to cleanliness, all with a critical eye. With AI tools like ChatGPT, you can streamline your efforts by generating checklists, report templates, and detailed feedback narratives. By combining AI resources with your keen sense of observation, you can deliver valuable insights that businesses use to improve their customer experience.

How to Use AI Tools:

- **Evaluation Checklists**: Use ChatGPT to create comprehensive, detailed checklists tailored to the specific business or service being evaluated.
- **Report Templates**: Develop structured report templates to capture all observations clearly and consistently.
- **Scenario Questions**: Generate conversation starters and specific questions to guide interactions with staff during your visits.
- **Customer Experience Metrics**: Use AI to brainstorm creative ways to assess less obvious aspects of the overall customer experience.

Potential Earnings:

- $7 - $20+ per assignment, depending on complexity, duration, and experience level.

Platforms to Use:

- **BestMark:** A variety of mystery shopping opportunities across multiple industries.
- **Market Force:** Specializes in retail and restaurant evaluations.
- **IntelliShop:** Offers a diverse selection of mystery shopping assignments.

Quick-Start Steps:

1. **Sign Up**: Join trusted mystery shopping companies and complete their registration or training.
2. **Develop Skills**: Practice your memory and observation skills to capture every detail during visits.
3. **Stay Organized**: Set up a system for tracking assignments, deadlines, and submitting reports.
4. **Focus on Objectivity**: Keep personal biases out of your evaluations to provide businesses with accurate, factual feedback.

Tips for Success:

- **Tailor AI Checklists**: Use AI-generated checklists as a baseline but stay flexible, allowing for unexpected observations.
- **Blend In**: The key to being a great mystery shopper is maintaining your role as a regular customer – don't draw attention to yourself.
- **Stay Factual**: Your reports should be objective and detail-focused, relying on concrete facts rather than personal opinions.
- **Follow Instructions**: Pay close attention to the specific guidelines for each assignment to ensure your feedback meets company requirements.

Mystery shopping requires delivering authentic, unbiased insights while remaining discreet. AI can enhance your evaluations by keeping them organized, but the real value comes from your keen observation and ability to report what businesses truly need to know. Maintaining integrity, respecting confidentiality, and continuously refining your attention to detail are essential. Focusing on industries you understand and perfecting your feedback style can turn mystery shopping into a rewarding side hustle that helps shape customer experiences.

96. Errand Running

Errand running might seem simple, but it's a lifeline for busy individuals and businesses that need a helping hand with their daily tasks. Whether you're picking up groceries, waiting for deliveries, or running to the post office, you have the opportunity to make people's lives easier and less stressful. AI tools like ChatGPT can take your service to the next level, planning efficient routes, organizing tasks, and ensuring seamless communication with your clients. Combining your organizational skills and reliability with AI-generated resources, you can offer a time-saving, stress-relieving service that clients will appreciate.

How to Use AI Tools:

- **Optimized Route Plans**: Use ChatGPT to create the most efficient route for completing multiple errands in one trip.
- **Custom Checklists**: Develop detailed checklists for each type of errand, ensuring nothing gets missed.
- **Client Communication**: Create templates for quick, professional updates and confirmations with clients.
- **Service Ideas**: Generate creative ideas for additional errand services, like pet care or personal shopping.

Potential Earnings:

- $20 - $35+ per hour plus mileage, depending on the task complexity and your location.

Platforms to Use:

- **TaskRabbit**: For connecting with clients who need various tasks completed.

- **Nextdoor:** Ideal for finding local errand running gigs in your neighborhood.
- **Your own website or social media**: To attract direct clients and build a loyal customer base.

Quick-Start Steps:

1. **Define Services**: Decide which errands you're comfortable offering (e.g., grocery shopping, deliveries, waiting services).
2. **Set Pricing**: Create a pricing structure that reflects your time, travel, and task difficulty.
3. **Set Up Profiles**: Join task-based platforms or build your own website to market your services.
4. **Stay Organized**: Use task management apps and AI-generated checklists to keep track of multiple errands and clients.

Tips for Success:

- **Stay Flexible**: Use AI-generated plans for efficiency but adapt to last-minute changes and client requests.
- **Build Trust**: Establish a reputation for reliability and excellent communication with clients.
- **Master Time Management**: Juggle multiple errands effectively by keeping a strict schedule and using route optimization tools.
- **Stay Organized**: Use digital tools to track tasks, manage appointments, and maintain clear communication with clients.

As an errand runner, your role is to simplify life for others, and AI tools can assist you by helping you organize and complete tasks more efficiently. But ultimately, it's your dedication, reliability, and personal touch that clients will appreciate most. By focusing on trust and time management, you can build a thriving business, specializing in specific errands or offering niche services to stand out. Networking within your community and keeping up with local events can help you find new clients and maintain a steady stream of work.

97. Home Organizing

Have you ever walked into a cluttered space and felt that itch to transform it into a calm, organized oasis? Home organizing might be your calling! Helping others create functional, beautifully arranged spaces can significantly impact their daily lives. By using AI tools like ChatGPT, you can take your skills even further, creating personalized organization plans, custom inventory systems, and innovative storage ideas. Combining your creativity, problem-solving abilities, and AI-driven resources, you can provide home organization services that refresh your clients and inspire them in their newly optimized spaces.

How to Use AI Tools:

- **Room-Specific Checklists**: Use ChatGPT to create tailored organizing checklists for each room or space.
- **Custom Inventory Systems**: Develop detailed systems for categorizing and tracking items like clothes, books, and kitchen supplies.
- **Decluttering Strategies**: Generate personalized decluttering techniques that suit each client's lifestyle and habits.
- **Storage Solutions**: Come up with creative ideas for maximizing space and implementing unique storage solutions.

Potential Earnings:

- $30 - $130+ per hour, or $50 - $1,500 per project, depending on the complexity and your experience.

Platforms to Use:

- **Thumbtack:** For connecting with local clients seeking organizing services.
- **Houzz:** Ideal for showcasing your home organizing projects and attracting new business.
- **Instagram** or **Pinterest:** Build a visual portfolio to share before-and-after transformations and attract clients.

Quick-Start Steps:

1. **Build Organizing Skills**: Familiarize yourself with popular organizing methods (e.g., KonMari, SPACE) and techniques.
2. **Create a Portfolio**: Start with your home or a friend's space to document before-and-after transformations.
3. **Set Up Profiles**: Join platforms like Thumbtack or create your own website to promote your services.
4. **Network Locally**: Connect with real estate agents, interior designers, or community groups for potential clients.

Tips for Success:

- **Personalize Plans**: Use AI-generated checklists as a starting point, but tailor them to each client's unique needs and habits.
- **Focus on Long-Term Solutions**: Create organizing systems that clients can easily maintain.
- **Communication is Key**: Develop clear, empathetic communication skills to fully understand your client's needs.
- **Stay Current**: Keep up with the latest in organizing tools, products, and techniques to offer the best solutions.

Helping clients declutter and organize their homes is more than just aesthetics – creating spaces that enhance their lives. AI can streamline and improve the process, but your attention, creativity, and emotional understanding make the difference. Specializing in niche areas like small space organizations or working with specific client types, such as busy professionals or families, can help you stand out. Keep honing your skills, network with professionals in adjacent fields, and explore new ways to help your clients feel at peace in their organized, functional spaces.

98. Cleaning Services

Keeping a space clean and organized can do wonders for a person's well-being. If you love the satisfaction of seeing a space transform from cluttered to spotless, providing cleaning services could be the perfect fit for you! With AI tools like ChatGPT, you can elevate your cleaning business by creating efficient cleaning schedules, generating service checklists, and even organizing eco-friendly cleaning methods. Blending AI resources with your attention to detail and commitment to cleanliness allows you to offer thorough, personalized services that keep your client's homes and offices looking their best.

How to Use AI Tools:

- **Cleaning Checklists**: Use ChatGPT to generate room-by-room checklists for different types of spaces.
- **Customized Schedules**: Create tailored cleaning schedules that fit each client's needs, whether weekly, bi-weekly, or monthly.
- **Inventory Management**: Develop systems to track and manage your cleaning supplies.
- **Eco-Friendly Solutions**: Generate ideas for using sustainable and non-toxic cleaning products that are safe for both clients and the environment.

Potential Earnings:

- $20 - $50+ per hour for residential cleaning, or $40 - $100+ per session for specialized cleaning services.

Platforms to Use:

- **Handy:** For connecting with residential and commercial cleaning gigs.
- **Care.com:** For finding local residential cleaning jobs.
- **Nextdoor:** Ideal for finding local cleaning gigs in your neighborhood.
- **Your own website**: To attract clients directly through local advertising and networking.

Quick-Start Steps:

1. **Choose Your Niche**: Decide which cleaning services you want to offer (residential, commercial, specialized, etc.).
2. **Gather Supplies**: Invest in high-quality cleaning products and tools that will help you deliver exceptional results.
3. **Create a Pricing Structure**: Develop clear pricing based on the size of the space and the type of cleaning service provided.

4. **Promote Your Services**: Set up profiles on cleaning platforms or launch your own website to connect with potential clients.

Tips for Success:

- **Tailored Checklists**: Use AI-generated checklists as a foundation, then personalize them for each client's requirements.
- **Consistency is Key**: Maintain a high level of detail and consistency in every cleaning job.
- **Time Management**: Build strong time management skills to maximize your productivity and manage multiple clients effectively.
- **Stay Current**: Keep up with the latest cleaning techniques, products, and safety standards to deliver the best service possible.

Offering high-quality cleaning services requires more than elbow grease – it demands reliability, professionalism, and a personal touch. AI can help streamline your processes, but your commitment to each client's unique needs will set you apart. Build trust by using safe, effective cleaning products, respecting your clients' property, and delivering consistent results. As you gain experience, consider specializing in certain cleaning services like eco-friendly options or post-construction cleaning. Keep learning and networking to ensure your business continues to thrive and evolve.

99. Handyperson Services

When it comes to fixing things around the house or tackling repair projects, having someone reliable and skilled makes all the difference. If you have a knack for solving problems and enjoy hands-on work, offering handyperson services could be the perfect way to put your skills to good use. With AI tools like ChatGPT, you can take your business to the next level by streamlining job estimates, creating customized maintenance plans, and offering clients more efficient, well-organized services. Combining AI resources with your practical know-how ensures that your clients receive top-notch service, no matter the task.

How to Use AI Tools:

- **Job Estimation Templates**: Use ChatGPT to generate detailed estimates based on materials, time, and labor.
- **Maintenance Checklists**: Create customized checklists for regular home maintenance tasks tailored to each property.
- **Troubleshooting Guides**: Develop step-by-step guides for everyday household repairs or issues to help diagnose problems quickly.
- **Upselling Opportunities**: Generate ideas for suggesting additional services that complement the job you're hired for.

Potential Earnings:

- $50 - $100+ per hour, depending on the tasks' complexity and your expertise level.

Platforms to Use:

- **TaskRabbit:** To connect with local homeowners in need of handyperson services.
- **Angi:** A platform that helps you find new clients and showcase your reviews.
- **Nextdoor:** Great for finding local handyperson gigs in your neighborhood.
- **Your own website**: For direct marketing and client acquisition through local SEO and referrals.

Quick-Start Steps:

1. **Assess Your Skills**: Identify the range of services you can offer, from small repairs to larger home improvement projects.
2. **Get Licensed**: Ensure you have the necessary certifications or licenses, depending on your location and services.
3. **Invest in Tools**: Purchase quality tools that will allow you to handle various jobs.
4. **Build a Portfolio**: Document your work with before and after photos to showcase your expertise.

Tips for Success:

- **Customized Estimates**: Use AI-generated templates to create professional, accurate estimates but adapt them based on client-specific needs.
- **Clear Communication**: Keep clients informed about job details, costs, and timelines to build trust and avoid misunderstandings.
- **Expand Your Network**: Build relationships with other professionals for tasks that fall outside your expertise, like electrical or plumbing work.
- **Stay Informed**: Keep up with local building codes, safety regulations, and the latest tools and materials to ensure your work is up to standard.

AI may enhance your organization and efficiency, but clients will genuinely appreciate your skills, problem-solving abilities, and attention to detail. Reliability, transparency, and a commitment to high-quality work will help build a reputation as a trusted handyperson. To stand out, consider specializing in areas like carpentry, tiling, or exterior repairs. By consistently improving your trade and focusing on exceptional customer service, you'll create a thriving handyperson business that clients will return to again and again.

100. Moving Services

Moving can be one of life's most stressful experiences, but with the right help, it doesn't have to be. If you have the strength, organizational skills, and a knack for making the complicated simple, starting a moving service might be the perfect fit for you. With AI tools like ChatGPT, you can take your business to the next level by generating customized moving plans, creating efficient packing strategies, and ensuring smooth transitions for your clients. Combine these AI resources with your personal touch to provide reliable, stress-free moving services that make a real difference.

How to Use AI Tools:

- **Customized Moving Checklists**: Use ChatGPT to generate detailed checklists tailored to specific types of moves, from apartments to offices.
- **Inventory Tracking**: Create systems to keep track of clients' belongings throughout the move, ensuring nothing is left behind.
- **Optimized Loading Plans**: Develop strategies to load moving trucks efficiently, maximizing space and ensuring safe transport.
- **Cost Estimation Templates**: Generate cost estimation tools that offer transparency and help clients budget for their move.

Potential Earnings:

- $40 - $80+ per hour for two movers, or flat rates based on the size and distance of the move.

Platforms to Use:

- **U-Haul's Moving Helper:** For finding local moving gigs and gaining clients.
- **Thumbtack:** Connect with people looking for moving services in your area.
- **Nextdoor:** Ideal for finding local moving gigs in your neighborhood.
- **Your own website**: Use local SEO and advertising to attract clients directly.

Quick-Start Steps:

1. **Scale of Services**: Determine whether you'll focus on residential moves, long-distance relocations, or commercial jobs.
2. **Equipment**: Invest in essential tools like dollies, straps, and moving blankets to ensure the safety of your clients' belongings.
3. **Insurance and Licenses**: Ensure you're covered with the appropriate insurance and licenses required in your area.

4. **Pricing**: Create a transparent pricing structure that fits local market rates and the services you offer.

Tips for Success:

- **Tailored Plans**: Use AI-generated plans as a guide, but customize them based on individual client needs for a personal touch.
- **Care and Efficiency**: To minimize damage and maximize customer satisfaction, focus on careful handling of belongings and efficiency in loading/unloading.
- **Clear Communication**: Develop strong communication skills to keep clients informed throughout the moving process.
- **Organization**: Stay on top of logistics with digital scheduling tools and inventory management systems.

In the moving industry, the key to success is in the details – careful handling, clear communication, and excellent customer service. AI can boos efficiency and planning, your hands-on care and ability to manage challenges in real-time will set you apart. Specializing in niche areas like moving antiques, artwork, or heavy items like pianos can help you command higher rates and build a reputation for expertise. Keep honing your packing, logistics, and customer service skills to ensure smooth, positive experiences for every client.

101. Personal Shopping

Imagine helping clients find their perfect outfits, gifts, or must-have items, all while using your eye for style and creativity. Personal shopping could be your ideal side hustle if you love shopping and have a keen sense of trends and client preferences. With AI tools like ChatGPT, you can take your personal shopping services to the next level by generating style guides, curating gift lists, and creating efficient shopping strategies. Combine AI-generated insights with your fashion expertise and unique flair to deliver an unforgettable shopping experience that saves your clients time and ensures they always find the best items.

How to Use AI Tools:

- **Personalized Style Guides**: Use ChatGPT to generate tailored style guides that match each client's preferences and fashion goals.
- **Gift Idea Lists**: Create thoughtful gift idea lists based on occasions, recipient types, and client input.
- **Product Comparison Charts**: Develop comparison charts to help clients weigh product options based on price, quality, and features.
- **Shopping Itineraries**: Generate customized shopping itineraries for in-store or online shopping trips to save time and keep things efficient.

Potential Earnings:

- $28 - $44+ per hour, depending on your expertise and the shopping you specialize in.

Platforms to Use:

- Instacart: For grocery shopping and delivery gigs.
- Stella & Dot: For grocery shopping and delivery gigs.
- **Your website or social media**: Build a direct client base and showcase your unique style.

Quick-Start Steps:

1. **Define Your Niche**: Choose whether you'll focus on fashion, gifts, or specialty items like home decor.
2. **Knowledge of Brands**: Stay up-to-date on trends, brands, and product pricing in your chosen niche.
3. **Portfolio**: Build a portfolio or create social media profiles that show off your shopping expertise.
4. **Networking**: Build relationships with retailers and potential clients to grow your business.

Tips for Success:

- **Refine AI Suggestions**: Use AI-generated content as inspiration, but add your expert touch based on client feedback and experience.
- **Understand Client Needs**: To make shopping personalized, focus on getting to know each client's style, budget, and preferences.
- **Stay Updated**: Keep on top of the latest fashion trends, product launches, and seasonal sales.
- **Negotiate for Deals**: Develop great negotiation skills to ensure clients get the best value for their purchases.

In personal shopping, the key is to blend your knowledge of products, trends, and client preferences with your creativity. AI can help streamline your work, but clients truly value your personal connection and expertise. Make sure to stay informed about new fashion movements, retail shifts, and customer service best practices. Whether you focus on sustainable fashion, luxury shopping, or specialized gift buying, continuously improving your skills and staying connected with industry trends will help you stand out in this exciting field.

You did it!

Congratulations on reaching the end of this exciting journey into the world of AI-powered side hustles! As you've discovered, there are endless possibilities for combining your passions, skills, and AI tools to create profitable and meaningful ventures. Whether you're diving into creative fields like personal shopping or event planning or exploring tech-driven opportunities like transcription services or voiceover work, AI offers a powerful way to streamline your efforts and maximize your potential.

Remember, while AI can enhance and optimize your work, your unique expertise, creativity, and personal touch make a difference. Embrace the possibilities, continue learning and growing, and most importantly, enjoy building a side hustle that brings you financial success and fulfillment. Now, it's time to take action and make your side hustle dreams a reality – because with the right tools and mindset, there are no limits to what you can achieve!

Your Feedback Matters!

"For it is in giving that we receive."

St. Francis of Assisi

Before we dive into the exciting bonus section and wrap up with some final thoughts, we want to take a moment to thank you for joining us on this journey through *The Ultimate ChatGPT and Dall-E Side Hustle Bible*. By exploring these pages, you've already taken meaningful steps toward unlocking the powerful potential of AI-powered side hustles. We hope the ideas, strategies, and insights have sparked your creativity, motivation, and ambition to take action.

This is just the beginning. As you continue, remember that every side hustle explored here has the potential to evolve and grow in ways you may not have imagined yet. The tools are in your hands – now it's time to create something extraordinary.

If this book has inspired you, challenged you, or given you the confidence to start your own AI-powered side hustle, we would be incredibly grateful if you could take a moment to leave a review. Your feedback helps others discover the possibilities in these pages and helps us continue creating valuable content for aspiring entrepreneurs like you.

How to Leave a Review:

- Visit the platform where you purchased this book – Amazon, Goodreads, or any other store.
- Share your thoughts – What inspired you? What side hustles or strategies stood out? How has this book shaped your outlook on AI-powered side hustles?
- Help future readers – Your experience could inspire and guide someone else as they begin their own journey.

Why Your Review Matters:

Your review is more than just a reflection on this book – it's a way to help others find their path. Whether it's an aspiring side hustler or a seasoned entrepreneur, your feedback can motivate someone else to start or refine their AI-driven venture.

We're excited about what lies ahead, and there's still more to explore! Thank you again for reading. Let's continue the journey together.

With gratitude,
The FutureFront Team

Bonus
100 More AI-Assisted Side Hustle Ideas at a Glance

"Opportunities don't happen, you create them."

Chris Grosser

You thought we were done? Think again! As the world of AI continues to evolve, so do the opportunities for innovative side hustles. This bonus chapter provides a quick overview of 100 additional side hustle ideas, each with a brief suggestion for AI assistance and recommended platforms to get started. These ideas are designed to ignite your imagination and help you explore new possibilities for AI-powered entrepreneurship. Remember, these are just starting points – use your creativity to expand on them, and always consider the ethical implications and the need for human oversight when leveraging AI tools.

1. **Rental Property Management** (AI for tenant screening, maintenance scheduling) - Platforms: Zillow, Airbnb Co-host
2. **Drone Services** (AI for image processing, flight planning) - Platforms: DroneDeploy, Fiverr, Upwork
3. **Meal Prep Services** (AI for recipe generation, nutritional analysis) - Platforms: MealPro, HelloFresh
4. **Car Detailing** (AI for appointment scheduling, service customization) - Platforms: Mobile Tech RX, Detailing Success
5. **Home Staging** (AI for virtual staging, design suggestions) - Platforms: BoxBrownie, VirtualStaging.com
6. **Personal Chef** (AI for menu planning, ingredient sourcing) - Platforms: HireAChef, Thumbtack
7. **Mobile Notary** (AI for document verification, appointment scheduling) - Platforms: Notarize, DocVerify
8. **Airbnb Experience Host** (AI for itinerary creation, pricing optimization) - Platform: Airbnb
9. **Bike Repair** (AI for diagnostics, inventory management) - Platforms: Bike Repair App, Velofix
10. **Computer Repair** (AI for troubleshooting, parts sourcing) - Platforms: Geek Squad, HelloTech
11. **Furniture Flipping** (AI for price estimation, style trend analysis) - Platforms: Facebook Marketplace, Chairish
12. **Calligraphy Services** (AI for font suggestion, layout design) - Platforms: Etsy, Fiverr

13. **Tarot Card Reading** (AI for interpretation suggestions, client tracking) - Platforms: Keen, Kasamba
14. **Composting Service** (AI for optimal compost mix suggestions, pickup scheduling) - Platforms: CompostNow, Recyclebank
15. **Eco-Friendly Product Consultant** (AI for product recommendations, impact analysis) - Platforms: EcoEnclose, Grove Collaborative
16. **Genealogy Research** (AI for data mining, family tree visualization) - Platforms: Ancestry.com, MyHeritage
17. **AI-Generated Art Curation** (Curating and selling AI-created artworks) - Platforms: ArtStation, Foundation
18. **Scrap Metal Collection** (AI for price tracking, route optimization) - Platform: iScrapApp
19. **Aquarium Maintenance** (AI for water quality analysis, feeding schedules) - Platforms: Marineland, Chewy
20. **Holiday Decorator** (AI for design suggestions, inventory management) - Platforms: Thumbtack, TaskRabbit
21. **Professional Line Waiter** (AI for wait time estimation, client matching) - Platform: Same Ole Line Dudes
22. **Mobile Car Washing** (AI for appointment scheduling, water usage optimization) - Platform: Washos
23. **Knife Sharpening** (AI for edge analysis, appointment scheduling) - Platforms: KnifeAid, SharpeningSupplies.com
24. **Personal Stylist** (AI for outfit suggestions, size predictions) - Platform: Stitch Fix
25. **Urban Farming Consultant** (AI for crop planning, yield prediction) - Platforms: UrbanLeaf, Infarm
26. **Jingle Writing** (AI for melody generation, lyrics suggestions) - Platforms: Fiverr, AirGigs
27. **Trivia Host** (AI for question generation, difficulty calibration) - Platforms: Kahoot!, Quizizz
28. **Mobile Locksmith** (AI for lock diagnostics, inventory management) - Platform: 1-800-Unlocks
29. **Balloon Artist** (AI for design suggestions, pricing optimization) - Platforms: Etsy, GigSalad
30. **Caricature Artist** (AI for facial feature analysis, style suggestions) - Platforms: Fiverr, GigSalad
31. **Mobile Oil Change Service** (AI for appointment scheduling, inventory management) - Platforms: YourMechanic, Wrench
32. **Party Planner** (AI for theme suggestions, budget optimization) - Platforms: Eventbrite, The Bash
33. **Resume Writing** (AI for keyword optimization, format suggestions) - Platforms: Resume.io, Zety
34. **College Application Consultant** (AI for essay analysis, school matching) - Platform: CollegeVine
35. **Soap Making** (AI for recipe formulation, scent combination) - Platforms: Etsy, Shopify
36. **Candle Making** (AI for scent profiling, burn time prediction) - Platforms: Etsy, Amazon Handmade

37. **Custom Embroidery** (AI for design digitization, thread color suggestion) - Platforms: Etsy, Printful

38. **Appliance Repair** (AI for diagnostics, parts sourcing) - Platforms: Angi, HomeAdvisor

39. **Carpet Cleaning** (AI for stain analysis, treatment recommendation) - Platforms: Thumbtack, HomeAdvisor

40. **Window Washing** (AI for job quoting, route optimization) - Platforms: TaskRabbit, Handy

41. **Gutter Cleaning** (AI for job estimation, scheduling optimization) - Platforms: Thumbtack, HomeAdvisor

42. **Snow Removal** (AI for weather prediction, route optimization) - Platform: Plowz & Mowz

43. **Lawn Care** (AI for grass health analysis, mowing patterns) - Platforms: LawnStarter, GreenPal

44. **Pet Grooming** (AI for breed-specific grooming suggestions, appointment scheduling) - Platforms: Rover, Wag!

45. **Mobile Mechanic** (AI for diagnostics, parts sourcing) - Platforms: YourMechanic, Wrench

46. **Personal Trainer** (AI for workout planning, progress tracking) - Platforms: Trainerize, My PT Hub

47. **Meditation Guide** (AI for personalized meditation suggestions, mood tracking) - Platforms: Insight Timer, Calm

48. **Yoga Instructor** (AI for pose sequencing, alignment checking) - Platforms: Yoga International, Glo

49. **Dance Instructor** (AI for choreography suggestions, music matching) - Platforms: Steezy, DancePlug

50. **Golf Caddy** (AI for club selection, course analysis) - Platforms: 18Birdies, GolfNow

51. **Sports Referee** (AI for rule checking, game analysis) - Platforms: RefReps, Referee.com

52. **Gaming Coach** (AI for strategy analysis, player performance tracking) - Platforms: Gamer Sensei, Fiverr

53. **Twitch Streamer** (AI for content scheduling, audience engagement) - Platform: Twitch

54. **LEGO Designer** (AI for model suggestions, piece inventory) - Platforms: Bricklink, Rebrickable, Lego

55. **Custom Toy Creator** (AI for design suggestions, safety compliance) - Platforms: Etsy, Shapeways

56. **3D Printing Service** (AI for model optimization, print time estimation) - Platforms: Shapeways, Treatstock

57. **Vinyl Cutting and Crafting** (AI for design suggestions, material optimization) - Platforms: Etsy, Cricut

58. **Personalized Gift Baskets** (AI for product pairing, theme suggestions) - Platforms: Etsy, GiftBasket.com

59. **Custom Phone Case Designer** (AI for trend analysis, design generation) - Platforms: Printful, Redbubble

60. **Vintage Clothing Reseller** (AI for authenticity checking, pricing optimization) - Platforms: Depop, Poshmark

61. **Antique Appraiser** (AI for item identification, market value estimation) - Platforms: WorthPoint, ValueMyStuff

62. **College Textbook Reseller** (AI for price tracking, condition analysis) - Platforms: TextbookRush, Chegg
63. **Dumpster Rental Service** (AI for size recommendation, scheduling optimization) - Platforms: Dumpsters.com, Budget Dumpster
64. **Parking Lot Striping** (AI for layout optimization, paint usage estimation) - Platforms: Angi, HomeAdvisor
65. **Pressure Washing** (AI for surface analysis, water usage optimization) - Platforms: Thumbtack, PressureWashingResource
66. **Graffiti Removal** (AI for removal method suggestion, job quoting) - Platforms: Angi, HomeAdvisor
67. **Pool Maintenance** (AI for water chemistry analysis, cleaning scheduling) - Platforms: Poolzenia, Poolsmith Technologies
68. **Chimney Sweep** (AI for cleaning method suggestion, scheduling optimization) - Platforms: Angi, HomeAdvisor
69. **Radon Testing** (AI for risk assessment, mitigation planning) - Platforms: Angi, HomeAdvisor
70. **Home Energy Auditor** (AI for energy loss detection, improvement suggestions) - Platforms: Energy Sage, HomeAdvisor
71. **Solar Panel Cleaner** (AI for cleaning schedule optimization, performance analysis) - Platforms: Angi, SolarReviews
72. **Septic Tank Service** (AI for maintenance scheduling, problem diagnosis) - Platforms: Angi, HomeAdvisor
73. **Pest Control** (AI for pest identification, treatment planning) - Platforms: Thumbtack, Orkin
74. **Beekeeping and Honey Production** (AI for hive health monitoring, honey yield prediction) - Platforms: Etsy, Local Honey Finder
75. **Goat Rental for Lawn Clearing** (AI for grazing area calculation, herd size optimization) - Platforms: Hiregoats.com, Angi
76. **Mobile Pet Grooming** (AI for breed-specific grooming plans, route optimization) - Platforms: Rover, Wag!
77. **Dog Walking** (AI for route planning, pack matching, advertising) - Platforms: Rover, Wag!
78. **Pet Waste Removal** (AI for route optimization, schedule planning) - Platforms: DoodyCalls, Poop 911
79. **Aquarium Design and Maintenance** (AI for ecosystem balance, fish compatibility) - Platforms: Thumbtack, HomeAdvisor
80. **Custom Aquarium Building** (AI for design optimization, material calculation) - Platforms: Angi, CustomAquariums
81. **Terrarium Designer** (AI for plant pairing, care scheduling) - Platforms: Etsy, Shopify
82. **Closet Organizer** (AI for space optimization, style categorization) - Platforms: Thumbtack, Houzz

83. **Garage Organization Specialist** (AI for space planning, inventory management) - Platforms: Thumbtack, HomeAdvisor

84. **Attic and Basement Cleanout Service** (AI for item valuation, disposal planning) - Platforms: Angi, 1-800-GOT-JUNK

85. **Junk Hauling** (AI for load estimation, route optimization) - Platforms: ReadyRubbishRemoval.com, 1-800-GOT-JUNK

86. **Estate Sale Organizer** (AI for item valuation, pricing strategy) - Platforms: EstateSales.net, EstateSales.org

87. **Professional Mourner** (AI for eulogy generation, emotion simulation) - Platforms: MyWillandWishes.com, Fiverr

88. **Ride Share Driver** (AI for optimized route planning, real-time traffic updates) – Platforms: Uber, Lyft

89. **Tour Guide** (AI for route planning, fact-checking) - Platforms: ToursByLocals, Viator

90. **Packing and Unpacking Service** (AI for box organization, inventory management) - Platforms: TaskRabbit, Unpakt

91. **Furniture Assembly** (AI for instruction interpretation, tool suggestion) - Platforms: TaskRabbit, Handy

92. **Wallpaper Installation** (AI for pattern matching, material calculation) - Platforms: Angi, HomeAdvisor

93. **Custom Curtain Making** (AI for fabric suggestion, measurement calculation) - Platforms: Etsy, Houzz

94. **Upholstery Cleaning** (AI for fabric analysis, cleaning method suggestion) - Platforms: Thumbtack, Angi

95. **Boat Cleaning and Detailing** (AI for cleaning product selection, job quoting) - Platforms: Boatyard, GetMyBoat

96. **RV Winterizing Service** (AI for procedure customization, appointment scheduling) - Platforms: RVShare, Outdoorsy

97. **Firewood Delivery** (AI for volume calculation, route optimization) - Platforms: Firewood Scout, Angi

98. **Christmas Tree Delivery and Setup** (AI for tree selection, decoration suggestion) - Platforms: TaskRabbit, Thumbtack

99. **Holiday Light Installation and Removal** (AI for design planning, energy consumption estimation) - Platforms: Thumbtack, HomeAdvisor

100. **New Year's Resolution Coach** (AI for goal setting, progress tracking) - Platforms: Coach.me, Fiverr

This extensive list shows AI's limitless potential for enhancing and diversifying your side hustle options. Whether you're looking to boost your current business or dive into something entirely new, there's something here for everyone. As you explore these additional ideas, keep a growth mindset, remain adaptable, and let your unique skills and creativity guide you. The key is not just to start but to stay open to learning and evolving along the way. Each side hustle is an opportunity to harness AI and shape a successful and rewarding future.

Conclusion
Embracing the AI-Powered Future of Side Hustles

"Believe you can and you're halfway there."

Theodore Roosevelt

As we reach the end of this exploration into AI-powered side hustles, it's clear that we stand at the threshold of a new era in entrepreneurship. The fusion of human creativity with artificial intelligence has blown the doors wide open, revealing once unimaginable opportunities. From content creation to data interpretation, from AI-assisted art to innovative problem-solving, AI is fundamentally transforming how we approach side hustles and redefining the boundaries of what's possible.

Throughout this journey, we've laid a solid foundation, exploring core concepts of AI technology and its practical applications in side hustles. We've delved into the entrepreneurial mindset, understanding that success in this new frontier requires creativity, resilience, and adaptability.

At the heart of our exploration were 101 innovative ideas for AI-powered side hustles. These ideas represent the intersection of human ingenuity and AI capabilities, offering potential launchpads for your entrepreneurial journey. We've seen how AI enhances traditional side hustles, making them more efficient and scalable while creating entirely new work categories that never existed before.

But ideas alone aren't enough. That's why we also explored how to turn these concepts into reality, from setting up your workspace to navigating the financial considerations of running an AI-enhanced business. We addressed challenges like pricing, marketing, and client management in this brave new world of AI-assisted work.

As we conclude, remember that the true power of AI in side hustles lies not in the technology itself but in how you apply it. The real magic happens when AI is combined with your unique experiences, skills, creativity, and perspectives. These elements will set your AI-powered side hustle apart in a competitive marketplace. The ideas in this book aren't rigid blueprints but springboards for your imagination and innovation.

As you embark on your own AI-powered side hustle journey, keep these fundamental principles in mind:

- **Embrace continuous learning:** AI is evolving at a breakneck pace. What's cutting-edge today may be obsolete tomorrow. Cultivate a mindset of curiosity and lifelong learning. Stay informed about new developments, experiment with emerging tools, and never stop expanding your knowledge base.
- **Start small, think big:** While having ambitious goals is important, remember that every successful venture starts

with small steps. Begin with manageable projects that allow you to learn and grow, but always keep your long-term vision in sight. Let each small success fuel your journey towards bigger achievements.

- **Prioritize ethical practices:** As you leverage the power of AI, remember the importance of ethical considerations. Prioritize transparency in your use of AI, ensure fairness in your practices, and always respect privacy and data protection. Building trust with your clients and customers is paramount in the AI era.
- **Balance automation with the human touch:** While AI can dramatically enhance efficiency and capabilities, never underestimate the value of your human insights and creativity. The most successful AI-powered side hustles find the sweet spot between leveraging AI's strengths and showcasing uniquely human qualities.
- **Be adaptable:** The landscape of AI and side hustles will continue to evolve. What works today may need to be refined or completely reimagined tomorrow. Cultivate flexibility in your approach and be willing to pivot when necessary. Your ability to adapt may well be your most valuable asset.
- **Focus on problem-solving:** The most successful side hustles, AI-powered or otherwise, solve real problems for real people. Always focus on the value you're providing to your clients or customers. Let AI enhance your ability to address their needs effectively and efficiently.
- **Build a supportive network:** Entrepreneurship can be a solitary journey, but it doesn't have to be. Connect with other AI enthusiasts and side hustlers. Share experiences, learn from each other's successes and failures, and collaborate when possible. Your network can be a source of support, inspiration, and opportunities.
- **Maintain work-life balance:** The flexibility of side hustles can be both a blessing and a curse. While AI can help automate many tasks, setting boundaries and avoiding burnout is crucial. Remember, the goal of a side hustle is to enhance your life, not consume it.

AI is reshaping the future of work, and side hustles are at the forefront of this transformation. By embracing these changes, you're diversifying your skills and positioning yourself at the forefront of the new economy. You're joining a movement redefining how we work in the 21st century.

Starting a side hustle can feel both exciting and daunting. Remember, every successful entrepreneur once stood where you are now – with an idea and the courage to pursue it. The path may not always be smooth, but it will be filled with growth, innovation, and reward.

Your unique blend of skills, combined with AI, opens up a world of limitless possibilities. The only question is: What will you create? How will you leave your mark on this AI-powered future?

As you close this book, we encourage you to take that first step. Choose an idea that resonates with you. Start small, dream big, and begin your journey with confidence. The tools and knowledge you need to succeed are now in your hands.

The world of AI-powered side hustles isn't just waiting for your contribution – it needs it. Your unique perspective and creativity are critical ingredients for the next breakthrough. The future is AI-powered, and you now have the tools to shape it. Your next adventure, your path to financial freedom and personal fulfillment, begins now.

So, take a deep breath, embrace the excitement of the unknown, and step forward. The world of AI-powered side hustles is full of potential – and it's waiting for you.

Go forth and hustle. Your AI-powered future starts today!

Your AI Side Hustle Resource Hub

"The future belongs to those who learn more skills and combine them in creative ways."
Robert Greene

Your "AI Side Hustle Resource Hub" is a carefully curated list of valuable links and tools mentioned throughout the book. We've compiled them here for easy reference and access.

If you're reading the eBook version, all the links throughout the book are clickable, allowing you to easily access tools and resources as you read. However, if you're reading the print version, the links aren't clickable, so we've created an external resource hub for your convenience.

For eBook readers, feel free to revisit this section anytime to quickly find all the helpful resources mentioned in earlier chapters. For print readers, simply scan the QR code provided to open a clickable PDF with all the resources in one easy-to-access document.

We've included this hub to enhance your reading experience and provide ongoing value as you explore and implement AI side hustle ideas. **In addition, you'll find 101 helpful articles offering inspiration and insight, categorized by each side hustle mentioned in the book.**

Explore these resources at your own pace, and don't hesitate to revisit this hub as you progress through different stages of your AI side hustle adventure.

Click the link **here** or use the QR code below:

Side Hustle Index

"The secret of getting ahead is getting started."

Mark Twain

The following index lists all the side hustles featured in this book by number. If you are reading a print copy, use this guide to quickly navigate opportunities that resonate with your skills and interests. If you read as an eBook, you can navigate each section by clicking on the title. Whether you're exploring creative paths, financial strategies, or service-based options, each section offers practical insights to help you succeed in your side hustle journey.

Listed by Side Hustle Number

Writing & Content Creation

Art & Design

Marketing & Advertising

Digital Products & Services

Education & Training

Finance & Investment

Customer Service

Miscellaneous

References

10 Unique Ways Freelance Insurance Agents Can Elevate Their Business. (n.d.). Copywriter Collective. Retrieved September 20, 2024, from https://copywritercollective.com/freelance-insurance-agents/

2024 Guide to Tutor Earnings: Strategies for Maximizing your tutoring income. (n.d.). https://workee.net/blog/maximizing-earnings-strategic-guide-to-tutor-pay-in-2024

A Step-By-Step Guide on How to Become a Wedding Officiant. (n.d.). The Penny Hoarder. Retrieved September 20, 2024, from https://www.thepennyhoarder.com/make-money/side-gigs/how-to-become-a-wedding-officiant/

Abdallah, M. (2022, September 20). *How much to charge for email marketing freelance: Guidelines for Freelancers.* Moe Abdallah. https://moeabdallah.com/blog/how-much-to-charge-for-email-marketing-freelance/

Addis, K. (2024, September 16). How to make money blogging: the complete free guide. *Wix Blog.* https://www.wix.com/blog/how-to-make-money-blogging#:~:text=Within%20the%20first%20year%2C%20bloggers,%24500%2D%242%2C000%20per%20month.&text=As%20you%20can%20see%2C%20you,re%20not%20a%20professional%20writer.

Admin. (2024, February 7). *How I broke into technical writing—and why you should too.* Mediabistro. https://www.mediabistro.com/go-freelance/journalism-advice/technical-writing/

Aleksey. (n.d.). *How to sell posters online (step-by-step).* Sellfy. https://blog.sellfy.com/sell-posters-online/

App Developer Salary Guide (2024). (2024, September 12). Business of Apps. https://www.businessofapps.com/app-developers/research/ios-android-developer-salary/#:~:text=Overall%20independent%20app%20developers'%20average,generate%20on%20average%20%2444%2C000%20monthly.

Arvin, L. (2024, June 7). How much does a logo designer usually get paid? *Kreafolk.* https://kreafolk.com/blogs/articles/how-much-logo-designer-get-paid

Attié, I. (2024, September 17). *Shutterstock contributor review.* Stock Photo Secrets. https://www.stockphotosecrets.com/stock-agency-insights/shutterstock-contributor-review.html#:~:text=Contributors%20earn%20a%20base%20rate,portfolio%20size%2C%20and%20performance%20level

Beehiiv. (2024, February 9). *beehiiv Blog.* Beehiiv Blog. https://blog.beehiiv.com/

Bestmark. (2024, July 9). How much does mystery shopping pay? | BestMark. *BestMark.* https://www.bestmark.com/news/mystery-shopping/articles/how-much-does-mystery-shopping-pay/

Bilingual Customer Support Specialist Salary. (n.d.). Ziprecruiter. Retrieved September 20, 2024, from https://www.ziprecruiter.com/Salaries/Bilingual-Customer-Support-Specialist-Salary

Blackbyrn, S. (2024, June 4). How to become a debt management coach? - Coach Foundation. *Coach Foundation*. https://coachfoundation.com/blog/how-to-become-debt-management-coach/

Blanckenberg, N., & Blanckenberg, N. (2024, May 7). *Building a 7-figure business selling posters online [in 6 steps]*. https://blog.storeya.com/2020/06/selling-posters-online/

Blinco, S. (2023, June 16). *House sitting and retirement – 9 years of freedom*. Travel Live Learn. https://www.travellivelearn.com/house-sitting-and-retirement/

BostonSpeaks: Turning Public Speaking into a Six-Figure Business on Kajabi. (n.d.). https://kajabi.com/creator-stories/kit-pang-boston-speaks

Buha, L. (2024, August 9). *Cleaning business success stories to inspire you*. Trafft. https://trafft.com/cleaning-business-success-stories/

business entrepreneur. (2023, October 17). Your path to success in the personal shopper business. *Medium*. https://medium.com/@entrepren-eurbusiness/your-path-to-success-in-the-personal-shopper-business-10c16d5c3880

Bute, J. (2024, May 28). How much money can custom T-Shirts make? *Printify*. https://printify.com/blog/how-much-money-can-custom-t-shirts-make/

By. (2024, June 13). *How to write a killer press release (and what to charge)*. The Freelancer's Year. https://thefreelancersyear.com/blog/how-write-press-release-and-what-to-charge/

Care.com. (2023, January 20). *Pet sitting cost: How much should I pay a pet sitter?* Care.com Resources. https://www.care.com/c/en-ca/pet-sitting-cost-how-much-should-i-pay-a-pet-sitter/

Christison, C. (2024, May 29). *How much do freelance social media managers make in 2024?* Social Media Marketing & Management Dashboard. https://blog.hootsuite.com/freelance-social-media-manager/

Chung, W. (2024, September 16). *Domain Flipping: What it is and how to get started*. Hostinger Tutorials. https://www.hostinger.com/tutorials/domain-flipping#How_Much_Money_Can_You_Make_from_Domain_Flipping

Consumer Experience Consultant Salary. (n.d.). Ziprecruiter. Retrieved September 19, 2024, from https://www.ziprecruiter.com/Salaries/Consumer-Experience-Consultant-Salary

Cost of tax accountants 2024 | How much are average tax preparation fees | Bark. (2024, March 18). Bark.com. https://www.bark.com/en/us/tax-accountants/cost-of-tax-preparation/#:~:text=Hourly%20Rates%20for%20Tax%20Preparation,their%20additional%20certification%20and%20expertise.

Council, B. (2024, September 17). *How to become a cryptocurrency consultant? [UPDATED] - Blockchain Council*. Blockchain Council. https://www.blockchain-council.org/cryptocurrency/how-to-become-a-cryptocurrency-consultant/

Customer feedback jobs. (n.d.). Ziprecruiter. Retrieved September 19, 2024, from https://www.ziprecruiter.com/Jobs/Customer-Feedback

Customer Service Representative Salary. (n.d.). Ziprecruiter. Retrieved September 20, 2024, from https://www.ziprecruiter.com/Salaries/Customer-Service-Representative-Salary

Customer Service Training Specialist Salary. (n.d.). Ziprecruiter. Retrieved September 19, 2024, from https://www.ziprecruiter.com/Salaries/Customer-Service-Training-Specialist-Salary

Cv-Manager. (2024, September 2). *How much money do resume writer make?* Executive Resume Writing for C-Suite Executives.
https://c-suitecvsecure.com/blog/post/how-much-money-do-resume-writer-make#:~:text=Average%20Earnings,%24400%20per%20resume%20or%20more.

Decker, A. (2024, April 17). The Ultimate Guide to Training for Customer Service & Support. *Hubspot*. Retrieved September 20, 2024, from https://blog.hubspot.com/service/customer-service-support-training

Dyksterhouse, L. (2024, March 25). *How to make money as a freelance videographer*. Videomaker. https://www.videomaker.com/how-to/profitmaking/promotion/how-to-make-money-as-a-freelance-videographer/

EasyWebinar. (2024, April 16). *Do You Know The Average Earnings Per Webinar - Let's Find Out*. EasyWebinar. https://easywebinar.com/earnings-potential-of-webinars/#:~:text=Additionally%2C%2065%25%20of%20marketers%20earn,appeals%20to%20your%20target%20audience.

Fitzwater, A. (2024, May 22). *Side hustles for music teachers*. Yamaha Music - Blog. https://hub.yamaha.com/music-educators/learn-peers/case-studies/side-hustles/

Freelance illustration rates: The complete guide to pricing your work. (2022, January 17). Creative Boom. https://www.creativeboom.com/tips/freelance-illustration-rates/

Freelance software developer Salary and jobs: How to get started. (2022, May 26). https://www.profitablefreelancer.com/freelance-software-developer-salary-and-jobs-what-to-expect-and-how-to-get-started

Freshworks. (2024, April 11). *Multilingual customer support: ultimate guide*. Freshworks. https://www.freshworks.com/customer-service/support/multilingual/

Fueled. (2024, May 22). *How much money can you earn with an app in 2024? | Fueled*. https://fueled.com/blog/much-money-can-earn-app/

Gardner, A. (2024, July 9). *Make Money proofreading: 18 best Online proofreading jobs in 2024*. Millennial Money Man. https://millennialmoneyman.com/make-money-proofreading/

Goodey, B. (n.d.). *Customer Feedback Analysis: Step-By-Step + Template*. https://www.sentisum.com/customer-feedback-analysis

Hamer, A. (2024, September 19). *How to become a video content creator in 2024*. https://www.descript.com/blog/article/how-to-earn-money-as-a-video-content-creator#:~:text=You%20can%20earn%20money%20through,can%20deter%20them%20over%20time.

Hamilton, J. (2024, January 30). *How much do ghostwriters make? Common rates.* Kindlepreneur. https://kindlepreneur.com/how-much-do-ghostwriters-make/#:~:text=your%20book%20now-,Ghostwriting%20Can%20Be%20Lucrative,%2415%2C000%20to%20%2440%2C000%2B%20per%20book

Hire technical talent quickly - Get matched in 48 hours. (n.d.). https://www.usebraintrust.com/hire/community-managers#:~:text=On%20average%2C%20a%20Community%20Manager,%2420%20to%20%24100%20per%20hour.

Hourly Rates. (n.d.). Upwork. Retrieved September 19, 2024, from https://www.upwork.com/guides/hourly-rates

Hourly rates for freelance CRM Specialists Freelance Rates - Rate Calculator. (n.d.). Thirdwork: Freelance Talent for the Best Crypto Startups. https://www.thirdwork.xyz/rate-guides/Hourly-rate-for-crm-specialist-freelancers

How I made $93K in revenue selling digital downloads on Etsy | Amma Rose Designs blog. (n.d.). https://ammarosedesigns.com/how-to-i-made-93k-in-revenue-selling-digital-downloads-on-etsy/

How Much Can You Make with a Membership Site? (n.d.). Brilliant Directories. Retrieved September 20, 2024, from https://www.brilliantdirectories.com/blog/how-much-can-you-make-with-a-membership-site#:~:text=Consider%20a%20site%20focused%20on,looking%20at%20%2415%2C000%20per%20month.

How Much To Pay a House Sitter: Average Rates (2024). (n.d.). Urbansitter. Retrieved September 20, 2024, from https://blog.urbansitter.com/how-much-to-pay-a-house-sitter/#:~:text=According%20to%20the%20Economic%20Research,between%20%2425%2C500%20and%20%2438%2C500%20annually.

How to Be a Wallpaper Designer. (n.d.). Skillshare. Retrieved September 20, 2024, from https://www.skillshare.com/en/blog/how-to-be-a-wallpaper-designer/

How to Become a Branding Consultant in 4 Steps (With Skills). (n.d.). Indeed. Retrieved September 20, 2024, from https://ca.indeed.com/career-advice/finding-a-job/branding-consultant

How to succeed in virtual customer service field - A complete guide. (n.d.). https://www.pitchnhire.com/blog/virtual-customer-service

https://www.cmc-canada.ca. (n.d.). *Demystifying Customer Experience: A guide for consultants.* Consult by CMC-Canada. https://www.cmc-canada.ca/consult/demystifying-customer-experience-a-guide-for-consultants

IanGriffin. (2013, January 25). *Interview with a Freelance Speechwriter - Job Shadow.* Job Shadow. https://jobshadow.com/interview-with-a-freelance-speechwriter/

Indy. (2024, January 15). Copywriting for Beginners: How to start earning money. *Indy.* https://weareindy.com/blog/copywriting-for-beginners-how-to-start-earning-money

I've Used Paid Online Survey Sites to Earn Extra Money – Here's How to Get Started. (n.d.). Usnews.com. https://money.usnews.com/money/personal-finance/family-finance/articles/paid-online-survey-sites-that-will-earn-you-extra-money

Jo, H. (2024, June 2). *5 best platforms for a travel Agent side hustle.* NanoWhat. https://nanowhat.com/5-best-platforms-for-a-travel-agent-side-hustle/

Kagan, J. (2023, June 20). *Retirement Planner: Who They are, What They do.* Investopedia. https://www.investopedia.com/terms/r/retirement-planner.asp

Krawczyk, N. (2024, September 9). *How much do copywriters actually make?* Filthy Rich Writer. https://filthyrichwriter.com/how-much-do-copywriters-make/

Kurichenko, V., & Kurichenko, V. (2024, August 9). How to make money from SEO 2024 (Even if you are a beginner). *Self Made Millennials -*. https://selfmademillennials.com/how-to-make-money-from-seo/

LearnVest. (2021, June 30). How I made "4,000 a year mystery shopping. *Forbes.* https://www.forbes.com/sites/learnvest/2013/03/01/how-i-made-14000-a-year-mystery-shopping/

LeDonne, R. (2023, March 9). *How to break into podcast writing.* The Freelance Creative. https://contently.net/2023/02/23/trends/writing-for-podcasts/

Lerner, M. (2024, May 15). *12 best websites to teach languages online and make $30 an hour easily — Sololingual.* Sololingual. https://www.sololingual.com/blog/teaching-languages-online

Lloyd, L. (2024, February 26). How much do professional organizers charge? *Forbes Home.* https://www.forbes.com/home-improvement/cleaning-organization/professional-organizer-cost/

Loper, N. (2024, July 9). *Online Focus Groups: Up to >50/hr Paid Research Studies (2024).* Side Hustle Nation. https://www.sidehustlenation.com/consumer-research-companies-online-focus-groups/

Main, K. (2024, July 25). *PPC Advertising: The Ultimate Guide.* Forbes Advisor. https://www.forbes.com/advisor/business/ppc-marketing-guide/

Malekos, N., & Malekos, N. (2024, June 3). *How much do life coaches make in 2024.* LearnWorlds. https://www.learnworlds.com/how-much-life-coaches/

Maliha. (2024, August 29). *How to sell Canva templates & Make money on the side – a beginner's guide.* The Side Blogger. https://www.thesideblogger.com/how-to-sell-canva-templates/

Man consults for crowdfunding campaigns after successfully raising $4 million | Side hustle School. (n.d.). Side Hustle School. https://sidehustleschool.com/episode/220/

McGinley, C. (2023, November 17). Community Managers: What They Do & How to Be a Great One. *Hubspot.* Retrieved September 20, 2024, from https://blog.hubspot.com/marketing/great-community-management-tips

Miki, S. (2024, February 6). *Becoming a legal consultant: What you need to know.* Clio. https://www.clio.com/blog/how-to-become-a-legal-consultant/#:~:text=A%20legal%20consultant%20advises%20clients, minimize%20risks%20and%20achieve%20goals.

Mishra, A. (2024, March 21). What is the average cost of a stock trading coach? - Anand Mishra - Medium. *Medium.* https://medium.com/@anandmishra6465/what-is-the-average-cost-of-a-stock-trading-coach-c2ef0ae881f8#:~:text=Hourly%20rates%20can%20range%20from,2.

Molomo, K. (2024, August 2). *Get paid to write articles: 17 sites that pay $75+ per post*. BloggingPro. https://www.bloggingpro.com/get-paid-to-write-articles/#gref

Money, J. (2022, August 11). *Side Hustle #60: I’m a Voice Over Actor!* Budgets Are Sexy. https://budgetsaresexy.com/make-money-voice-over-actor/

Ogletree, A. (2024, August 26). How much do movers cost in 2024? *Forbes Home*. https://www.forbes.com/home-improvement/moving-services/movers-and-packers-cost/

Omind, T. (2024, July 7). *Why 'Voice First' is Crucial in AI Customer Service | Omind*. https://www.omind.ai/blogs/conversational-ai-customer-service-voice#:~:text=The%20'Voice%20First'%20approach%20has,resolutions%20and%20higher%20customer%20satisfaction.

Party Planners Unite: Your guide to a successful event planning side g. (n.d.). Fud - the World's First Social Hustling Community. https://blog.joinfud.com/p/party-planners-unite-your-guide-to-a-successful-event-planning-side-gig

Payne, M. (2024, July 3). How much to charge for house cleaning: 2024 pricing guide. *FreshBooks*. https://www.freshbooks.com/hub/estimates/estimate-house-cleaning-jobs#:~:text=for%20event%20cleaning%3A-,Hourly%3A%20%2440%20to%20%24100%20per%20hour%20per%20cleaner,home%20size%20and%20effort%20required

Pearce, J. (2023, January 10). 5 steps to become a book writing Coach (+ pros and Cons). *Make a Living Writing*. https://makealivingwriting.com/book-writing-coach/

Pearce, J. (2024, June 12). Where to Sell Short Stories: 7 places that pay. *Make a Living Writing*. https://makealivingwriting.com/where-to-sell-short-stories/

Popovic, D. (2024, January 8). *How much does social media design cost?* https://www.manypixels.co/blog/social-media-design/cost

Pratt, M. K. (2015, July 22). *Tech experts rake in the cash by teaching online*. Computerworld. https://www.computerworld.com/article/1625982/tech-experts-rake-in-the-cash-by-teaching-online-2.html

Product Tester Salary. (n.d.). Ziprecruiter. Retrieved September 20, 2024, from https://www.ziprecruiter.com/Salaries/Product-Tester-Salary

Rachael. (2023, May 7). How to make "00k to $400k as a freelance content writer - Mighty Freelancer | The Business of writing. *Mighty Freelancer*. https://mightyfreelancer.com/how-to-make-100k-to-400k-as-a-freelance-content-writer/

Regulacion, J. (n.d.). *How much money can you make Dropshipping (2023 stats)*. https://www.dripshipper.io/blog/how-much-can-you-make-dropshipping

Reyzer, R. (2023, October 4). How to earn money by writing product descriptions. *Rafal Reyzer*. https://rafalreyzer.com/earn-money-with-product-descriptions/

Rodrigo, B. A. (n.d.). *Acadium*. https://acadium.com/blog/how-to-become-a-freelance-digital-marketer/

Rudy, L. (2024, August 21). Picture Perfect: 26 Top Side hustles for Photographers. *doola: Start your dream US business and keep it 100% compliant*. https://www.doola.com/blog/side-hustles-for-photographers/

Ryzhkov, A. (2023, August 19). *How to maximize earnings as a real estate consultant.* https://finmodelslab.com/blogs/profitability/real-estate-consulting-profitability

S, H. (2024, March 21). *How much money can you make on Shopify? A comprehensive guide.* HulkApps. https://www.hulkapps.com/blogs/shopify-hub/how-much-money-can-you-make-on-shopify-a-comprehensive-guide#:~:text=Intermediate%20sellers%2C%20with%20optimized%20stores,into%20six%20figures%20and%20beyond.

Salary.com. (n.d.-a). *Hourly wage for Personal Shopper | Salary.com.* https://www.salary.com/research/salary/listing/personal-shopper-hourly-wages

Salary.com. (n.d.-b). *Hourly wage for Real Estate Consultant | Salary.com.* https://www.salary.com/research/salary/posting/real-estate-consultant-hourly-wages

Sarker, M. (2024, March 17). Is website flipping profitable in 2024? *The Website Flip.* https://thewebsiteflip.com/guide/website-flipping/profitable/

Schwartz, B. &. E. (2020, October 28). *Do Wedding Photographers make a lot money?* Wedding Photography and Films. https://weddingphotographyandfilms.com/wedding-blog/do-wedding-photographers-make-a-lot-money

Sethi, R. (2024, August 2). *How much do content creators make in 2024? (+Tips to make $).* I Will Teach You to Be Rich. https://www.iwillteachyoutoberich.com/how-much-do-content-creators-make/#:~:text=a%20creator's%20salary.-,Platform,post%2C%20depending%20on%20their%20rate.

Side Hustle Nation. (2024, July 12). *Affiliate marketing as a side hustle: A legit way to make money online.* https://www.sidehustlenation.com/online-business/affiliate-marketing/

Siu, E. (2024, September 4). *Newsletter Business: Profitable & Engaging strategies.* Single Grain. https://www.singlegrain.com/blog/ms/newsletters-good-business/

Slack, A. (2024, July 22). *How to Become a Freelance Grant Writer with No Experience.* Side Hustles. https://sidehustles.com/how-to-become-a-freelance-grant-writer/

Spraul, T. (2024, May 13). *How to make money as an online fitness coach (25 ways) in 2024 | Exercise.com.* Exercise.com | Software to Grow Your Fitness Business. https://www.exercise.com/grow/how-to-make-money-as-an-online-fitness-coach/

Staff, G. (2022, September 7). *Hourly rates for academic freelance writers - Guru blog.* https://www.guru.com/blog/hourly-rates-for-academic-freelance-writers/

Staff, W. (2023, February 7). Web designer salary (and promotion information) for 2023. *Web designer salary (and promotion information) for 2023.* https://www.waveapps.com/freelancing/web-designer-salary#:~:text=Side%20hustle%20and%20freelance,from%20%2430%20%2D%20%2480%20per%20hour.

Stage 32 - Stage 32. (n.d.). Stage 32. https://www.stage32.com/blog/4-ways-to-make-money-as-a-screenwriter-2757

Stahl, T. (2024, January 25). *Marketing Analytics: What it is & Why it matters.* Semrush Blog. https://www.semrush.com/blog/marketing-analytics/?kw=&cmp=CA_SRCH_DSA_Blog_EN&label=dsa_pagefeed&Network=g&Device=c&utm_content=683768475042&kwid=dsa-2267597098541&cmpid=18361978716&agpid=153749

927502&BU=Core&extid=122594792571&adpos=&gad_source=1&gclid=Cj0KCQjwn9y1BhC2ARIsAG5IY-65xKG6BeSYVTjAhkSa4R7kGYpqbSF4tsClQAik5Vr5SpCRMGGVonMaAuoxEALw_wcB

Starter Story: Learn how people are starting successful businesses. (n.d.-a). https://www.starterstory.com/ideas/stock-trading-consultant/success-stories

Starter Story: Learn how people are starting successful businesses. (n.d.-b). https://www.starterstory.com/ideas/financial-advisor/success-stories

Starter Story: Learn how people are starting successful businesses. (n.d.-c). https://www.starterstory.com/ideas/virtual-assistant/success-stories

Starter Story: Learn how people are starting successful businesses. (n.d.-d). https://www.starterstory.com/ideas/pet-care-business/success-stories#1-woofie-s-3m-year

Starter Story: Learn how people are starting successful businesses. (n.d.-e). https://www.starterstory.com/ideas/transcribing-service-business/success-stories

Starter Story: Learn how people are starting successful businesses. (n.d.-f). https://www.starterstory.com/ideas/translation-service-business/success-stories

Starter Story: Learn how people are starting successful businesses. (n.d.-g). https://www.starterstory.com/ideas/data-entry-service-business/success-stories

Starter Story: Learn how people are starting successful businesses. (n.d.-h). https://www.starterstory.com/ideas/home-organizer/success-stories

Starter Story: Learn how people are starting successful businesses. (n.d.-i). https://www.starterstory.com/ideas/handyman-business/success-stories

Starter Story: Learn how people are starting successful businesses. (n.d.-j). https://www.starterstory.com/ideas/packers-movers-business/success-stories

StreamingVideoProvider. (2024, May 28). *How much money can you make selling online courses?* https://www.streamingvideoprovider.com/online-course-platform/how-much-can-you-make-selling-online-courses/#:~:text=An%20increasing%20number%20of%20creators,and%20sell%20top%2Dquality%20courses.

Support. (2022, August 18). *The Beginner’s Guide to Teaching Art Online*. How to Sell Art Online | Online Marketing for Artists. https://theabundantartist.com/teaching-art-online/

Taylor, A. (2021, July 12). *Book cover design business*. Rising Innovator. https://www.risinginnovator.com/2021/01/book-cover-design-business/

The Career Catch Up. (2024, June 12). *COACHING PACKAGES - The career catch up*. The Career Catch Up - Career and Life Coaching for Women. https://www.careercatchup.com/packages/

The Ultimate Guide to Coach Stock market Traders. (2023, August 23). Siddharth Rajsekar. https://siddharthrajsekar.com/the-ultimate-guide-to-coach-stock-market-traders/

UI Designers on Upwork cost >0–$40/hr. (n.d.). Upwork. Retrieved September 20, 2024, from https://www.upwork.com/hire/ui-designers/cost/

Velarde, O., & Velarde, O. (2024, September 13). *How to make money selling ebooks in 2024.* Visme Blog. https://visme.co/blog/sell-ebooks/#:~:text=Publishing%20your%20own%20ebook%20is,which%20should%20meet%20certain%20requirements.

Velora Studios, LLC. https://velora.com. (n.d.). *Love to cook? Try these 12 online food business ideas to make money online.* Heights Platform. https://www.heightsplatform.com/blog/love-to-cook-try-these-12-online-food-business-ideas-to-make-money-online

Wallin, C. (2020, August 10). *Can you really make >00 a day Running Errands - Senior Errand service.* Senior Errand Service. https://www.seniorerrandservice.com/can-you-really-make-200-a-day-running-errands/

Walls, P. (2024, September 6). *{{ num_templates }} Product Tester Success Stories [{{ current_year }}].* https://www.starterstory.com/ideas/product-tester/success-stories

What Does a Handyman Cost? [2024 Data]. (n.d.). Angi. Retrieved September 20, 2024, from https://www.angi.com/articles/what-are-common-handyman-prices.htm

What's the going rate for custom business card design? Charge for business card design explained. (n.d.). https://www.4over4.com/content-hub/stories/how-much-to-charge-for-business-card-design

WwwIdeoPl, I.-. (n.d.). *Customer Service application implementation step by step / Digitization blog | Project-based Software Development.* Ideo Software. https://www.ideosoftware.com/blog/customer-service-application-implementation-step-by-step,235.html

Your customer support side gig: Money making opportunities in gig work unveiled - Copiliot Careers. (n.d.). https://www.copilotcareers.org/blog-posts/customer-support-side-gig-money-making-opportunities-in-gig-work

Zhou, L. (2024, April 18). How Much Do Career Coaches Make? (Per hour & year). *Luisa Zhou.* https://luisazhou.com/blog/how-much-do-career-coaches-make/#how-much-career-coaches-charge

Made in the USA
Coppell, TX
30 November 2024

41278795R10109